Berlin

"The Berlin Residence" by Johann Friedrich Hennig (ca. 1800).

Guide to the most beautiful sights

Text by M. Freutel, Berlin

Kunstverlag Edm. v. König, Heidelberg/Dielheim

Contents

Berlin is one of the most fascinating and colorful cities in Europe, an exciting metropolis pulsating with energy, whose irresistible attraction has something almost magical about it. Here, old and new, tradition and modernity have attained a balance and harmony rarely to be found in other cities, so that Berlin seems to the visitor to be an apparently inexhaustible treasure trove of past and present. Its broad, tree-lined avenues, lovely parks, remarkable Baroque palaces and monuments are not only impressive sights but serve as a reminder that the city was once the seat of power of the Prussian kings and, later, the German Emperors.

With so much of interest to see and do, it's well worth taking your time on a visit to Berlin: lively markets, excellent museums, innumerable cafés (many with live music): these are just a part of the city's generous "palette." Also, Berlin is the only city in the world where you can find two of virtually everything (e.g., universities, City Opera Houses, National Galleries, zoos) in either half of the city – a consequence of the 28-year division of Berlin after the Second World War.

Today, this city of seemingly endless boulevards with 4 million inhabitants is one of the most-visited places in Europe, so that almost everyone has heard of such streets as the Kurfürstendamm and Unter den Linden. Whereas the former, located in the west part of the city, is a delightful shopper's paradise in the style of the Thirties and Fifties, the latter is actually Berlin's original main street running through the heart of the city. It's in Unter den Linden that we find such superb works of architecture as the classical Brandenburg Gate or K.F. Schinkel's Neue Wache.

In addition to its numerous impressive buildings and monuments, Berlin can boast a larger surface area of water and woodland than any other city in Europe, so that its lively pace and big-city flair are balanced by ample opportunities to take a relaxing break. A particular attraction is to take a trip on one of the pleasure boats on the River Spree, while a visit to the lovely woods around the picturesque lakes, the Wannsee and Müggelsee, is highly recommended.

In addition to its numerous impressive buildings and monuments, Berlin can boast a larger surface area of water and woodland than any other city in Europe, so that its lively pace and big-city flair are balanced by ample opportunities to take a relaxing break. A particular attraction is to take a trip on one of the pleasure boats on the River Spree, while a visit to the lovely woods around the picturesque lakes, the Wannsee and Müggelsee, is highly recommended.

During your stay in Berlin, it's worth striking up an acquaintance with local cuisine by visiting a few of the city's innumerable traditional restaurants and bars. Specialities include knuckle of park (Eisbein), hearty stews (Eintöpfe), "currywurst", weissbier with a shot of fruit cordial, and delicious pancakes (Pfannkuchen). Their mixture of pleasant surround-

Kaiser William Church of Remembrance.

ings and good food make the restaurants of the old part of Berlin ideal places to while away an hour or two.

Berlin has so much to offer that it is virtually impossible simply to set off and hope to see all of the sights in a day. Therefore, it's a good idea follow a planned tour as described in the following pages. By doing so, you will not only cover the most interesting features of the city but also get to known the Berliners and their life style.

Important Dates and Events in the History of Berlin

6th/7th century	First settlement by Slavs.
9th century	Oldest known Slavic castle near Köpenick.
928	King Henry I conquers Brandenburg, the castle of the Hevels.
948	King Otto the Great establishes the bishoprics of Havelsberg and Brandenburg.
983	An uprising leads to the reconquest of these territories by the Slavs.
1134	Albrecht "the Bear" is granted territories east of the Elbe as fiefs by Emperor Lothar III.
1157	Brandenburg is again conquered by the Askans. Albrecht "the Bear" becomes the first Margrave of Brandenburg.
1197	First mention of Spandau as a protectorate of the Askans.
1200	Foundation of the trading settlements, Berlin and Cölln.
1237	First documentary mention of Cölln.
1244	First documentary mention of Berlin.
1249	First mention of the Franciscan Monastery.
1251	Berlin is exempted from customs duty.
1280	Berlin mentioned as the site of the first margravial mint east of the Elbe.
1297	Founding of the Dominican Priory.
1307	Unification of Berlin and Cölln. This is soon followed by the construction of a joint city hall on the long bridge.
1319	The death of Margrave Waldemar marks the end of the dynasty of the Brandenburg Askans.
1323	King Ludwig "the Bavarian" grants the Mark Brandenburg to his son, Ludwig.
1325	During unrest in Berlin, the provost of Bernau is killed by a crowd. As a result, the city is excommunicated by the Pope.
1344	After protracted negotiations in Rome, the city is released from the ban of excommunication.
1345	General parliament (Landtag) of Brandenburg held in Berlin.
1359	Berlin becomes a member of the Hanseatic League.
1373	Emperor Karl IV visits Berlin.
1376/80	Fires destroy almost all of the city.
1411/15	Frederick VI of Hohenzollern is appointed governor of the Mark Brandenburg by Emperor Sigismund. At the Council of Constance, he is made Elector of Brandenburg.
1432	Berlin and Cölln join forces against the Elector.
1447	Berlin and Cölln rise in protest against the building of the Elector's castle.
1448	Berlin/Cölln becomes the capital of Brandenburg.

1470	The castle in Cölln on the Spree becomes the permanent seat of government and administration of the Electors.
1539	Joachim II becomes Protestant.
1576–1611	The plague claims the lives of at least 9000 citizens.
1618–1648	Thirty Years' War: Wallenstein (1628/30) and Gustavus Adolphus of Sweden visit Berlin.
1640–1688	Elector Frederick William, the "Great Elector," consolidates and extends the power of the Hohenzollerns and lays the foundations of the state of Brandenburg-Prussia with its capital in Berlin.
1658	Defensive fortification of the city.
1662	The construction of the Friedrich Wilhelm Canal establishes a direct link between Breslau and Hamburg. Serving as a port of transshipment, Berlin becomes an important trade center.
1685	The financial extravagance of the Hohenzollerns almost drives the city into bankruptcy. The situation is rescued by the shrewd decision (Edict of Potsdam) of the later King of Prussia, Frederick I, to offer refuge to fellow Protestants (Huguenots) fleeing from persecution in France.
1701	In Königsberg, Frederick III of Hohenzollern (1688–1713) crowns himself as king "in" Prussia.
1688	Founding of Friedrichstadt.
1696	Foundation of the Academy of Arts in Berlin.
1700	Foundation of the Academy of Sciences in Berlin.

The city coat-of-arms (1709) with the upright 'Berlin Bear'. The eagle and the division into three parts were retained.

1709	The towns of Berlin, Cölln, Friedrichswerder, Dorotheenstadt and Friedrichstadt are united and become the royal capital.
1710	Foundation of the Berlin Charité Hospital.
1713–1740	Reign of the so-called "Soldier King," Frederick William I. The Pleasure Garden (Lustgarten) becomes a parade ground. The army is expanded, and many barracks are built in the city.
1735	Construction of a 6-meter-high city wall, serving as a customs border and to prevent soldiers deserting.
1740–1786	Reign of Frederick the Great. Berlin becomes an important European capital, but does not escape unscathed from the numerous wars of the period.
1744	Revival of the Academy of Sciences.
1756–1763	Seven Years' War. Soviet and Austrian troops occupy Berlin.
1797–1840	Reign of Frederick William III.
1799	Foundation of the Academy of Architecture.
1806	Napoleon I in Berlin.
1809	First assembly of city councillors in Berlin.
1810	Foundation of the Friedrich Wilhelm University (now the Humboldt University of Berlin) by Wilhelm von Humboldt.
1811	Friedrich Ludwig Jahn opens the first German sports center in the Hasenheide.
1812	Reoccupation by the French.
1816	After the overthrow of Napoleon, the creation of Unter den Linden and the Tiergarten by the architects, Schinkel, Lenné, Tieck and Rauch, contributes decisively to Berlin's present form and appearance.
1826	Opening of the first (English) gasworks in Berlin.
1834	Setting up of the German Customs Union (Zollverein).
1838	Opening of the first railway from Berlin to Potsdam.
1840–1861	Reign of Frederick William IV.
1847	Meeting of the first Prussian state parliament (Landtag) in Berlin.
1848	18th March: 230 people die when the March Revolution in Berlin against the monarchy is suppressed. 22nd May: meeting of the Prussian National Assembly, which is dissolved on 5th December. 23rd August to 3rd September: first German Workers' Congress in Berlin.
1850	Opening of the Landwehr Canal.
1857	Owing to the mental illness of Frederick William IV, his brother, William, becomes Prince Regent.
1861–1888	Reign of King William I; after 1871, he is the German Kaiser (Emperor).
1861	The neighboring towns of Wedding, Moabit, Schöneberg, Tempelhof, Prenzlauer Berg and Friedrichshain are incorporated into the city of Berlin.

1862	Bismarck becomes Minister-President and Foreign Minister of Prussia.
1866	Founding of the North German Confederation with Berlin as its capital.
1867/68	Demolition of the city wall built in 1735.
1869	Foundation of the Social Democratic Workers' Party by August Bebel and Wilhelm Liebknecht.
1871	Establishment of the German Empire, with King William I as Kaiser.
1878	Anti-socialist laws aimed at suppressing the socialist movement.
1879	First electrified railway unveiled at the Berlin Industrial Exhibition in Moabit.
1881	First telephone company with 45 subscribers.
1882	Opening in Lichterfelde of the first electrified streetcar route in the world.
1888	Reign of Kaiser Frederick III lasting only 99 days.
1888–1918	Reign of Kaiser William II.
1890	Owing to public pressure, repeal of the anti-socialist legislation of 1878, which leads to the fall of Bismarck.
1900	Berlin's population reaches 1.9 million.
1902	First subway in Berlin.
1914	1st August: outbreak of the First World War. William II gives the order for general mobilization from the balcony of his palace in Berlin.
1917	Founding of the Universum Film Company (UFA).
1918	Abdication of William II; end of Hohenzollern rule; Karl Liebknecht declares a communist republic (Räterepublik) from the Eosander Portal of the Berlin Palace, while Philipp Scheidemann declares the republic from a window of the Reichstag building.
1919	November Revolution; murder of Karl Liebknecht and Rosa Luxemburg by officers of the Reichstag Regiment.
1924	First Radio Exhibition (Funkausstellung).
1929	World economic crisis; 600.000 unemployed in Berlin.
1930	First-ever rocket-powered flight in Berlin-Tegel.
1933	30th January: Hitler seizes power; the Reichstag is dissolved; the Nazis ban all other political parties. 27th February: burning down of the Reichstag; during the night of the fire, 1500 suspects arrested in Berlin. 21st March: in the Garnison Church in Potsdam, President Hindenburg officially places the government in Hitler's hands. 1st April: first boycott of Jewish shops. 10th May: burning of prohibited books on Opernplatz.
1934	Setting up of the People's Court.
1936	Start of the deportation of Jews from Berlin to concentration camps. The eleventh Olympic Games take place in Berlin.
1937	Berlin celebrates its 700th anniversary.

1938	9th November: in the so-called "Crystal Night," about 80 synagogues are destroyed in Berlin.
1939	Outbreak of the Second World War. Berlin's population at this time is about 4.3 million.
1940	First air attacks on the city (25th August).
1942	On 20th January at the Wannsee Conference, leading politicians, economists, scientists and generals of the Third Reich decide on "the Final Solution of the Jewish Question."
1943	In the Sportpalast, Goebbels calls for "total war."
1944	20th July: failure of the bomb plot to assassinate Hitler. 6th September: Hitler orders the setting up of a German territorial army (Volkssturm).
1945	With terrible losses, the Soviet army succeeds in capturing Berlin on 2nd May. Six days later, Hitler's generals sign the capitulation in Berlin-Karlshorst. On 8th May, American, British and, later (12th August), French troops enter Berlin. The city is divided into four sectors.
1946	The Allies authorize the election of a city council.
1947	On 25th February, the Allied Control Council (directive no. 46) officially dissolves the state of Prussia.
1948	Currency reform in the west sectors. 26th June: start of the blockade of West Berlin. 6th September: the escalating East-West conflict causes a split in the municipal authorities of Berlin. 30th November: setting up of new municipal authorities in the Soviet sector. Friedrich Ebert (the son of the former social-democratic President of Germany) becomes Lord Mayor of East Berlin.
1949	12th May: end of the blockade of West Berlin. 7th October: founding of the German Democratic Republic (GDR) with East Berlin as its capital.
1950	1st October: the constitution of West Berlin comes into force. Ernst Reuter becomes the first Lord Mayor of West Berlin.
1951	The 3rd World Youth and Student Games with about 25.000 participants from 104 countries take place in East Berlin – the first major international event in the city in the post-war period.
1953	17th June: widespread unrest in East Berlin and other cities in the GDR directed against the East German government.
1955	19th October: first working session of the West German parliament (Bundestag) in West Berlin.
1958	Berlin Crisis.
1961	13th August: start of construction of the Berlin Wall with a length of 161 kilometers. 25th August: First post-war Radio and TV Exhibition (Funkausstellung) in West Berlin. 24th September: opening of the new German Opera House in Bismarckstrasse in West Berlin.

1963	President J.F. Kennedy visits West Berlin. 17th December: first agreement concerning travel permits between West and East Berlin.
1964	In the treaty of friendship between the Soviet Union and the GDR, West Berlin is referred to for the first time as "an independent political entity." 1st December: introduction of compulsory currency exchange for visitors from the West in East Berlin and the GDR.
1967/68	Beginning of student unrest. Berlin becomes the center of the West European protest movement.
1971	After a 19-year interruption, the link between the telephone systems of East and West Berlin is re-established. 27th August: Germany's first post-war international Funkausstellung held in West Berlin.
1975	Opening of Berlin-Tegel Airport.
1982	Margaret Thatcher visits West Berlin.
1983	First meeting of the Lord Mayor of West Berlin (R. von Weizsäcker) and the head of the GDR government (Erich Honecker) in East Berlin.
1984	The administration of the GDR state railway transfers the West Berlin railway network into the hands of the authorities of West Berlin.
1987	Lavish celebrations in both halves of the city to commemorate Berlin's 750th anniversary.
1989	9th November: fall of the Berlin Wall.
1990	The last People's Assembly of the GDR votes for joining the Federal Republic of Germany (FRG).
1991	Berlin becomes the capital of the FRG.

A remaining section of the Berlin Wall.

Walking Tour of East Berlin

Pariser Platz, Brandenburg Gate, Unter den Linden

Located directly in the very heart of the city, **Pariser Platz** has always been the central axis between the east and west parts of Berlin. Until the start of the Second World War, Pariser Platz was one of the best-known and most expensive areas of the city. This was the site of the famous Adlon – at that time, an exclusive luxury hotel – while the nearby Wilhelmstrasse, which formerly contained many government buildings, is now (as it was during the time of the GDR) Berlin's **Embassy Quarter**.

If we turn to look westward, we see the most famous symbol of Berlin, the **Brandenburg Gate** (Brandenburger Tor). This is the only survivor of the 14 city gates that offered the only access to and from the city through the Zollmauer, the 6-meter-high city wall that served as a customs barrier. This city gate in the classical style was modeled on the Propylaea in Athens and was built by Carl Gotthard Langhans between 1788 and 1791. Only 2 years later did it reach its final form with the addition of the Goddess of Victory (Siegesgöttin) in a horse-drawn chariot, a work by Gottfried Schadow.

The Brandenburg Gate on Pariser Platz.

The four-horse chariot and Geddess of Victory on the Brandenburg Gate.

During the French occupation, Napoleon ordered the statue to be taken to Paris, and it was only restored to its original position after his overthrow in 1814. The gate itself was so badly damaged during the Second World War that it had to be rebuilt in 1956/57.

In 1647, more than a century before the completion of the Brandenburg Gate, the "Great Elector," Frederick William, ordered the construction of the impressive avenue, **Unter den Linden**. This served as a link between the electoral castle in the city (Stadtschloss) and the Tiergarten, a park which, at this time, lay outside of the city wall.

2 Comic Opera

Proceeding away from the Brandenburg Gate along Unter den Linden, we pass the **Embassy of the Soviet Federation** and, after a few hundred meters, we see to the right the **Comic Opera** (Komische Oper). This is located on the site of the **Unter den Linden Theater** built by Fellner in 1890/92 (from 1898 to 1945, called the **Metropol Theater**). Destroyed during the war, the building had to be completely reconstructed and modernized, and received a new facade in the style of the 1950s. Directors of this well-known theater have included Walter Felsenstein (1947–76) and Harry Kupfer.

Night view of Berlin's most famous boulevard: Unter den Linden.

 Comic Opera:
Main entrance: Behrenstrasse 55–57, 10117 Berlin
Box-office opening hours: Mon.–Fri. 11 a.m. to 7 p.m.;
Sun. 1 p.m. till 1^1/$_2$ hours befor starting
Box-office: Tel. 030–20260360
Information: Tel. 030–47021000

Comic Opera.

3 French Cultural Center

Continuing eastward along the right-hand side of Unter den Linden, we come to the **French Cultural Center** (Französisches Kulturzentrum) located about 50 meters beyond the display windows of the Comic Opera. Along with an extensive library, seminar rooms and a cinema/lecture theater, this cultural center also has a gallery, in which changing exhibitions of works by French artists can be seen.

French Cultural Center:
Unter den Linden 37, 10117 Berlin
Opening hours, Mon.–Fri. 11 a.m. to 7 p.m.
Tel. 0 30–2 29 10 20

French Cultural Center.

4 Friedrichstrasse, Metropol Theater

Leaving the French Cultural Center, we continue a short distance along Unter den Linden before turning left into **Friedrichstrasse**. Walking along this street, there is little to remind us that this was one of the most renowned shopping and business areas in Berlin at the time of the German Kaisers. Only on passing Friedrichstrasse Station, which is over 100 years old, do we get some idea of the importance of this street at the turn of the present century. On the right behind the station (Bahnhof), we see the **Metropol Theater**, formerly the **Admiral's Palace**. Opened in 1873/74 as the "Admiral's Garden Baths,", this was later converted into public swimming baths and an ice-skating rink.

In 1922, the upper storey was turned into a theater, which after the Second World War, was used for performances by the famous cabaret group, "Die Distel." Only in 1955 did this become the home of the Metropol Theater, whose original stage (now the site of the Comic Opera) was completely destroyed during the war. As early as the turn of the present century, the Metropol Theater enjoyed an international reputation for its revues, operettas and musicals.

Metropol Theater:
Friedrichstrasse 101–102, 10117 Berlin
Opening hours: Tues.–Sat. 11 a.m. to 7 p.m.,
Sun. 3 p.m. to 5 p.m., Tel. 030–20246117

Berlin-Friedrichstrasse Station by the River Spree.

Continuing along Friedrichstrasse, we cross the River Spree over **Weidendamm Bridge** before turning left into Schiffbauerdamm. It's only a few paces until we reach **Bertolt-Brecht-Platz** and the nearby theater, the **Berliner Ensemble**.

Formerly called the Theater am Schiffbauerdamm, this was constructed according to plans by the architect, H. Seeling, in 1891/92. The somewhat plain, unornamented exterior facade belies the remarkable late-Baroque decorations and fittings of the theater inside. It was here that the playwright, Bertolt Brecht, made theater history with the first performance of his "Threepenny Opera" in 1928.

But it was only 26 years later after his return from exile in America that Brecht, his wife, Helene Weigel-Brecht and some old friends founded the

The Berliner Ensemble Theater, with a statue of the playwright, Bertolt Brecht, in the foreground.

Berliner Ensemble. In 1954 they moved into the theater on Schiffbauerdamm. The Berliner Ensemble only became famous in the 1950s, for example with its performance of the "Caucasian Chalk Circle".

6 German Theater and Kammerspiele

Leaving the Berliner Ensemble, we turn right to continue along the Schiff-bauerdamm and then take the next turning to the right into Albrecht-strasse. After a couple of hundred meters, this leads left into Schumann-strasse, and soon after this junction, we reach the **German Theater** (Deut-sches Theater) and the smaller studio theater, the Kammerspiele.

Built in 1849/50 according to plans drawn up by Schinkel's student, E. Tietz, it was formerly called the **Friedrich-Wilhelmstädtisches Theater**, and its first decades were often overshadowed by the imminent threat of bankruptcy. Like many private theaters of the period, its survival involved frequent recourse to productions of popular operettas by composers such as Johann Strauss, Offenbach and Suppé. In 1883, it was renamed the German Theater (founded by Adolph l'Arronge), with the ambitious aim of playing a decisive role in the theatrical history of the city.

However, it was to be some years before – between 1905 and 1935 under the artistic direction of Max Reinhardt and Otto Brahms – this theater attained a genuine international reputation. It was the world-famous director of the German Theater, Wolfgang Langhoff, who gained an inter-

German Theater and Kammerspiele.

national reputation for the theater with his highly acclaimed production of German drama classics.

Back in 1927, the well-known theater critic, Herbert Ihering, remarked that, "no theater in Berlin has the same colorful wealth of actors," a view which is still shared by the majority of the city's theater-goers.

German Theater and Kammerspiele:
Schumannstrasse 13a, 10117 Berlin
Opening hours: Mon.–Fri. 12 a.m. to 6 p.m.
Box-office: Tel. 030–28 44 12 52 26
Information: Tel. 030–2 84 41 22 12 22

7 Friedrichstadtpalast

Leaving the German Theater, we return along Schumannstrasse and, after rejoining Albrechtstrasse, take the first left turning into Reinhardt-Strasse, which soon leads us back to Friedrichstrasse. Almost directly opposite we see the facade of the **new Friedrichstadtpalast**.

The Friedrichstadtpalast Theater on Friedrichstrasse.

Its predecessor, the **old Friedrichstadtpalast**, was erected in the middle of the last century, but its dilapidated condition necessitated its demolition in 1985. Initially, this housed Berlin's first large covered market; however, the attempt to emulate the "shopping atmosphere" popular elsewhere in Europe was so unsuccessful that it had to be closed 6 months later owing to the lack of custom. After 1874, the building was used almost exclusively as a venue for various types of entertainment. Thus, it was here that Berliners first enjoyed the sensational performances of the famous Russian **Circus Salamansky**. Soon after, the **Circus Renz** began its notable career in the Friedrichstadtpalast. In 1919, the architect, Hans Poelzig was commissioned by Max Reinhardt to convert the former covered market into a theater. Under Reinhardt's direction during the next 5 years, the Friedrichstadtpalast was to attain a firm place in the history of German theater. From the time of Reinhardt's departure in 1924 until its demolition in 1985 (it had been rebuilt in 1945), this theater was the venue of countless revues and popular shows.

The new Friedrichstadtpalast, which was opened in 1984, has managed to retain something of the flair of its predecessor. As well as its large auditorium with 1889 seats, it also holds a **"Small Revue"** every evening, with a bar that is furnished and fitted in the style and spirit of the 1920s.

New Friedrichstadtpalais:
Friedrichstrasse 107, 10117 Berlin
Opening hours:
Mo. 1 to 6 p.m., Tues.–Fri. 1 to 7 p.m., Sat./Sun. 2 to 7 p.m.
Tel. 0 30–23 26 24 74

8 Dorotheenstädtischer Cemetery and Brecht House

Leaving the Friedrichstadtpalast, we turn right and continue along Friedrichstrasse. After a couple of hundred meters, this street crosses Hannoverische Strasse and runs into Chausseestrasse. Here, on the left, we come to two adjoining graveyards (Friedhöfe), the **Französischer and Dorotheenstädtischer Cemeteries** located next to the **Brecht House**.

These cemeteries, which were laid out in the middle of the last century, are separated from the busy shops and traffic of this area by a high surrounding wall which ensures that they are literally "places of peace." The more famous of the two is the Dorotheenstädtischer Cemetery, owing to the number of graves of famous authors, philosophers and outstanding personalities to be found there. These include the philosophers, G.F.W. Hegel and J.G. Fichte and the architect, K.F. Schinkel, along with writers, musicians and inventors such as B. Brecht, his wife, H. Weigel-Brecht, J.R. Becher, A. Seghers, P. Dessau, H. Eisler, A. Zweig,

Dorotheenstädtischer Cemetery: Gravestone of the architect, Karl Friedrich Schinkel.

J. Heartfeld (the first person to use photomontage for political caricatures) and E. Litfass, the inventor of the round advertizing columns that are named after him in Germany (Litfass-Säule). Just next to the cemetery is the Brecht House built in the late-classical style, which was the home and workplace of B. Brecht and his wife, H. Weigel-Brecht, until their deaths in 1956 and 1971, respectively. It now houses the Center for Bertolt Brecht Research.

Brecht House Berlin:
Chausseestrasse 125, 10115 Berlin
Opening hours: Tues.–Fri. 10 to 12 a.m.,
(Thurs. 5 to 7 p.m.); Sat. 9.30 to 12 a.m. and 12.30 to 2 p.m.
Tel. 0 30–28 29 99 16

9 New Synagogue

Returning along Chausseestrasse and rejoining Friedrichstrasse, we turn into the next street on the left, Oranienburger Strasse. After a short walk of about 500 meters, we see the recently reconstructed **New Synagogue** on the left.

Built in the Moorish style in 1859–66 according to plans by E. Knoblauch and F.A. Stüler, the original synagogue had room for a congregation of about 3000. As in all Jewish places of worship, the building had separate sections for men and women. Standing in front of the facade with its gilded central cupola and side towers, it is not difficult to recognize the importance of Moorish elements in the building's remarkable design.

It was just three years before the Nazis seized power that this building received its most famous visitor; on 29th January, 1930, the man who devised the general theory of relativity, Albert Einstein, gave a violin concert here.

In the so-called **"Crystal Night," (9th November, 1938)**, the building was plundered and set on fire by the Nazis. A plaque recalls that, after 1942, the synagogue was used by the Fascists as a gathering point for about 500.000 Jews before their deportation to concentration and extermination camps. The fate of this outstandingly attractive building was sealed during the first bombing attacks of 1943, which reduced it to a complete ruin. Only in 1988 (during the GDR period) was a trust for the reconstruction of the synagogue finally set up. Today, the center houses an archive with library, a café and rooms for exhibitions and meetings.

The New Synagogue in Oranienburger Strasse.

New Synagogue:
Oranienburger Strasse 39, 10117 Berlin
Guided tours for individuals and groups by appointment only
Tel. 0 30–2 80 12 50

10 Sophienkirche

Leaving the New Synagogue, we continue along the left side of Oranienburger Strasse before taking the first left turn into Krausnickstrasse. This
leads on into Grosse Hamburger Strasse, which brings us directly opposite the entrance portal of the **Sophienkirche**. This simple hall church was
built in 1712, but its lovely tower was added only in 1892 (according to
plans of the architects, A. Heyden and A. Berndt), making it one of the
city's most attractive church buildings. In fact, the Sophienkirche has the
distinction of being the only Baroque church in Berlin. Its name is derived from its most generous patroness, Queen Sophie Luise.

Sophienkirche:
Grosse Hamburger Strasse 28, 10115 Berlin
Open all day
Tel. 0 30–2 82 32 32

11 Museum Island

Having visited the Sophienkirche, we follow the Grosse Hamburger
Strasse to the left until reaching Oranienburger Strasse. Turning left, we
follow this street until the streetcar station, Hackesche Markt. Just by
this, we turn right into the street, Am Zwinggraben, which we follow
(under the arches of the streetcar viaduct) until we come to Burgstrasse.
Turning left, we follow this street along the River Spree until we cross the
Friedrich Bridge on the right to reach Bodestrasse.
We have now arrived at the **Spree Island**, the location of one of the biggest museum complexes in the world, which was completed in 1830 following designs and plans drawn up by Schinkel. This unique group of five
museums resembling a collection of temples vividly recalls the buildings
of ancient Greece. The remarkable archeological treasures that have been
gathered here comprise one of the most extensive collections to be found
anywhere in Europe. A visit here is thus a marvelous opportunity to gain
insights into thousands of years of Mediterranean, Near Eastern, East
Asian, Indian and Islamic culture. In addition, there is a constantly
changing program of exhibitions of modern and traditional art and arte-
facts.

Following double-pages: The 'Museum Island' on the River Spree.

Immediately after crossing the Spree, we pass to the right into the garden of the **National Gallery**.

Constructed over a period of about 10 years (1866–76), this was designed by Stüler and was the second (after the Brandenburg Gate) major edifice of the city to be built of sandstone.

Flanked by a double flight of steps, this architectural masterpiece contains one of the most extensive collections of paintings to be found in Germany. Along with works by such German artists as Feuerbach and Menzel, French art is also well-represented by paintings by famous artists such as Manet, Degas and Courbet.

Old National Gallery – Bodestrasse entrance
Museumsinsel, Bodestrasse 1–3, 10178 Berlin
Tel. 0 30–20 90–50, Fax 0 30–20 90–63 70 – Opening hours:
Tuesday to Sunday, 9 a.m. to 5 p.m. Closed on Mondays.

National Gallery: E. Degas, "The Conversation" (ca. 1884).

Leaving the National Gallery, we see the **Old Museum** (Altes Museum) almost directly opposite. This is best approached from the spacious Lustgarten (Pleasure Garden) to the south, on which side the main entrance is located. This impressive construction in the Romantic-classical style could be said to be built "on stilts," as until its erection about 170 years ago, this site was actually a branch of the Spree. Indeed, for a long time, this part of the river served as a defensive moat, while historic drawings have shown that the city wall ran along what is now Bodestrasse.

The Old Museum adjoining the former Pleasure Garden (Lustgarten).

The recent unification of Germany has led to a good deal of rethinking with respect to the city's museums, the main idea being to bring back together certain collections that were previously on show separately in East and West Berlin. East and West Berlin, as the continually changing programme of exhibitions will show.

Old Museum – Lustgarten entrance
Museumsinsel, Bodestrasse 1–3, 10178 Berlin
Tel. 0 30–20 90 52 00, Fax 0 30–20 90 52 02
Opening hours: Tues.–Sun. 9 a.m. to 5 p.m.

Pergamon Museum – Kupfergraben entrance

This building was completed in 1930, and contains three different museums and collections (we will list the most interesting exhibits in each department – there is a plan at the entrance to the museum).

Antiquities collection: Pergamon altar, a masterpiece of Hellenic art in honour of Zeus (2nd century BC); the richly decorated market gate of Milet (2nd century AD); Greek and Roman sculptures; small *objets d'art* and mosaics.

Asia Minor Museum: processional road and Ishtar Gate from ancient Babylon, 580 BC (rooms 8 and 9); Asarhaddon's stele, 7th century BC (room 3); brick façade of the temple of the goddess Innana in Uruk (Sumerian culture); bas-relief from the palace of Assumersipal II in Kalchu, 9th century BC (rooms 10 and 11).

Museum of Islamic Art: façade of the Omalyadic castle of Mhatta (8th century), east of the Dead Sea; wall decoration from a house in Aleppo (early 17th century); miniature paintings (15th to 17th centuries).

Museumsinsel, Bodestr. 1–3, 10178 Berlin – Opening hours: Tuesday to Sunday, 9 a.m. to 5 p.m. Closed on Mondays. Also closed on 1st Jan., 24th, 25th, and 31st Dec. and on the Tuesdays after Easter Monday and Whit Monday:
Museum of Islamic Art
Tel. 0 30/20 90 54 01, Fax 0 30/20 90 54 02
Antiquities Collection
Tel. 0 30/20 90 52 00, Fax 0 30/20 90 52 02
Asia Minor Museum
Tel. 0 30/20 90 53 01, Fax 0 30/20 90 63 70

IId New Museum

Turning to the right, we can soon see part of the **New Museum** (Neues Museum) located behind the Old Museum and next to the National Gallery. In contrast to the four other museums on the island site, this building is characterized by a rather plain style. Completed in 1858, the New Museum was more severely damaged during the war than any of the other museums, so that its reconstruction was only begun in 1986. When work is complete, the **Museum of Prehistory and Early History** as well as the **Egyptian Museum** are to be housed here.

The Pergamon Museum on the Spree Canal.

e Bode Museum

The **Bode Museum**, which is located next to the Pergamon Museum further along the Kupfergraben canal, is also reached by crossing a bridge. Built between 1897 and 1904 by E. von Ihne, this building on the north tip of the Spree Island has the appearance of a floating fortress.

Formerly called the Kaiser Friedrich Museum, the Bode Museum was given its present name in 1958 in honor of its founder, Wilhelm von Bode (1845–1929), whose career in the city's cultural life spanned about half-a-century. His greatest achievements, though, occurred in the last 15 years of his life, during which time von Bode was in charge of building up the "museum landscape" of Berlin.

In addition to the **Egyptian Museum**, the **Bode Museum** also contains the **Museum of Late Classical and Byzantine Art**, a **Coin Collection** and the **Sculpture Collection.**

Information

Bode Museum – Monbijoubrücke entrance
Museumsinsel, Bodestrasse 1–3, 10178 Berlin
Tel. 030/20905–0
Tuesday to Sunday, 9 a.m. to 5 p.m. Closed on Mondays.

The Bode Museum on the northernmost tip of the 'Museum Island'.

Museum of Islamic Art in the Pergamon Museum: Aleppo Room (Syria, ca. 1600).

Leaving the Bode Museum, we turn left and return along Am Kupfergraben until this runs into the street, Am Giesshaus. Following the course of
this street to the right, we then turn right into the Festungsgraben, which
takes us past the Palais am Festungsgraben, behind which we come to the
main portal of the **Maxim Gorky Theater**.
Originally built as a School of Choral Music in 1825–27, the architecture
of this classical-style building was clearly much-influenced by Schinkel.
20th century authors form the core of the program of the Maxim Gorky
Theater. Maxim Gorky not only gave his name to this stage – his dramas
and works by other Soviet authors often feature in the theater's program.

Maxim Gorky Theater:
Am Festungsgraben 2, 10117 Berlin
Opening hours: Mon.–Sat. 1 to 6.30 p.m.; Sun. 3 to 6.30 p.m.
Tel. 0 30–20 22 11 29

3 **State Library of Berlin –**
Prussian Cultural Trust, House I

Passing the Maxim Gorky Theater on our left, we turn left into Clara-
Zetkin-Strasse. After less than 100 meters, we come to Hegelplatz, from
which we can see to the left the rear side and courtyard of the Humboldt
University of Berlin. From here, we continue a little further along Clara-
Zetkin-Strasse before taking the next left turning into Universitäts-
Strasse, which soon brings us back to Unter den Linden. Before turning
right toward the **State Library** (Staatsbibliothek), take a look at the middle of the avenue, which is dominated at this point by the Equestrian Statue of Frederick II, whose appellation, "the Great," had nothing to do
with his rather small physical stature. The work of Christian Daniel
Rauch, this monument was nearly 50 years in the making before it was
finally completed in 1851.
From here, it's a matter of a few paces before we reach the building hous-
ing the State Library (I), which was erected between 1903 and 1914 in
the neo-Baroque style according to plans of E. von Ihnes. The entrance
to the library itself is reached by crossing the lovely forecourt with its
attractive fountain. This monumental building contains about 3 million
volumes and no less than 3.5 million manuscripts, which can be perused
in the 12 reading rooms open to visitors.

State Library of Berlin – Prussian Cultural Trust, House I.

State Library of Berlin – Prussian Cultural Trust, House I
Unter den Linden 8, 10117 Berlin
Opening hours:
Mon.–Fri. 9 a.m. to 9 p.m.; Sat. 9 a.m. to 5 p.m.
Tel. 030–2015–0

14 Bebelplatz, Old Library

Coming out of the State Library, we cross Unter den Linden and go a short distance to our right before turning left into Charlottenstrasse. Following this until the next junction, we again turn left into Behrenstrasse, so that it's only a couple of hundred meters until we reach **Bebelplatz** and the **Old Library** (Alte Bibliothek) located to our left.

Formerly called the **Royal Library** and often nicknamed the "Chest of Drawers" (Kommode), this building was constructed between 1775 and 1780 according to a plan drawn up 50 years before by J.E. Fischer von Erlach for the Michael's Wing of the Court Castle (Hofburg) in Vienna. This perhaps explains its curious amalgamation of late Frederician architecture and the Viennese Baroque style. Under the supervision of the architect, G.C. Unger, the "new" Royal Library took only 5 years to build. In contrast, its Austrian "model" was only completed over a century later! At the time of its opening, the Royal Library contained about 150,000 books, and access was limited to the king himself and a few privileged persons.

Since 1914, it has served as the institute building of the Humboldt University of Berlin. The square in front of the Old Library – the former

Opernplatz – was chosen by the Nazis for a mass burning of prohibited books on 10th May, 1933.

The severe damage suffered by this building complex during the Second World War necessitated its almost complete reconstruction between 1967 and 1969.

Equestrian statue
Frederick II.
of Prussia.

5 Cathedral of St. Hedwig

Turning back toward Behrenstrasse, we see the main portal of the **Cathedral of St. Hedwig** on our left.

Built between 1747 and 1773 according to plans and sketches by Frederick II, J. Legeay and J. Boumann, this church has always been the diocesan church of the bishopric of Berlin.

The cathedral was almost entirely destroyed during the Second World War and was rebuilt between 1952 and 1963.

We return back along Behrenstrasse for a short distance before turning left into Markgrafenstrasse. From here, it's only a few paces to the **Gendarmenmarkt**.

The focal point of the group of classical-style buildings that we now have before us is the Schauspielhaus, a theater built according to plans drawn up by K. F. Schinkel. Severely damaged during the war, it required many years of painstaking reconstruction before the building was re-opened as the **Concert Hall** (Konzerthaus) in 1984.

To the north of the Concert Hall, we see another classical building, the **French Cathedral** (Französischer Dom). Built in the late-Baroque classical style, this church was constructed between 1701 and 1705 and was the work of the architects, J.L. Cayart and A. Quesnay. Formerly, the French Cathedral served as the main church of the Protestant Huguenot community, to whose history the museum now located inside the church is dedicated.

The former Schauspielhaus Theater and French Cathedral on the Gendarmenmarkt.

The Gendarmenmarkt attained its present form thanks to alterations made on the command of Frederick II, as a result of which, the German Cathedral (Deutscher Dom) was built (by M. Grünberg, 1701–08) as the counterpart of the French Cathedral directly opposite.

Huguenot Museum:
Gendarmenmarkt im Französischen Dom, 10117 Berlin
Opening hours: Weds.–Sat. 12 a.m. to 5 p.m.;
Sun. 1 to 5 p.m., Tel. 030–2291760

7 Friedrichswerdersche Church

Crossing Markgrafenstrasse, we now turn right into Jägerstrasse, the street than runs between the French Cathedral and the Concert Hall. We follow this street until it terminates in Oberwallstrasse. If we look straight ahead past the park, we see the gigantic former Headquarters of the Central Committee of the Socialist Party. Turning left, we soon come to a church made of brick, the so-called **Friedrichswerdersche Church**.
This building could be said to represent an effort to establish an architectural link between Gothic elements and the the principles of German clas-

The Friedrichswerdersche Church
now contains the Schinkel Museum.

sicism. Completed by K.F. Schinkel in 1830, this unusual masterpiece was (along with the Academy of Architecture destroyed during the war) one of the very first brick buildings to be constructed in Berlin. The main nave of the church now houses the **Schinkel Museum**, which recalls the life and works of the great architect.

18 Palais Unter den Linden

If we continue along Oberwallstrasse past the Friedrichwerderische Kirche, we reach Unter den Linden after passing through an archway. On the right, we come to a palace that takes its name from the city's most famous avenue.

This former residence of Crown Prince Frederick II was built in 1663 under the supervision of the architect, J.A. Nering. In 1732 on the commission of Frederick William I, the Crown Prince Palais was remodeled in the Baroque style, and about 80 years later, it was joined to the Princess Palais by the archway through which we have just passed. Unfortunately, the **Palais Unter den Linden** was one of the city's architectural gems that was almost utterly destroyed during the Allied bombing raids of the Second World War. As a result, the few remains of the palais were torn down in 1961, and with the help of historic drawings, the building was completely reconstructed under the supervision of the architect, R. Paulik, in 1968–69. It now belongs to the German government and is used for official receptions and other ceremonial occasions.

The above-mentioned palais which is joined to the Palais Unter den Linden by an archway is now called the **Opernpalais**.

This was built in 1733 by F.W. Diterich for the Prussian Minister of Finance, but after 1810 served as the permanent residence of princesses of the Prussian royal family.

Like its adjoining architectural counterpart, the Palais Unter den Linden, the Opernpalais was also a victim of air raids in the Second World War and was completely reconstructed in 1962–63.

Today, this impressive palais contains a café, a restaurant and a piano bar.

20 German State Opera

The German State Opera (Deutsche Staatsoper; located just past the popular Operncafé) is an opera house of international repute. Built in 1741–43 in the north-German Rococo-classical style, the **former Court Opera** (Hofoper) has the form of a Corinthian Temple and was designed by Knobelsdorff. Exactly one hundred years later (1843), the building was badly damaged in a fire and was reconstructed by C.F. Langhans. Further severe damage occurred during the Second World War, so that a

The German State Opera.

comprehensive reconstruction took place in 1955 under the supervision of K. Hemmerling and R. Paulick. The last major modernization of the German State Opera took place in 1986.

The long and distinguished history of this opera house includes the names of the composer/conductors, Richard Strauss and Giacomo Meyerbeer, as well as the singer, Maria Cebotari. The German State Opera is still one of the most popular theaters in Berlin.

German State Opera:
Unter den Linden 7, 10117 Berlin
Opening hours:
Mon.–Sat. 10 a.m. to 8 p.m.; Sun. 2 to 8 p.m.
Tel. 030–2035 4555, Fax 030–2035 4483

21 Humboldt University of Berlin

If we now cross Unter den Linden, we find ourselves almost directly in front of the main entrance of the **Humboldt University of Berlin**.
Built between 1748 and 1766 according to plans by Boumann as a palace for Prince Henry, this building became the home of Berlin University in 1809/10 thanks to the efforts of Wilhelm von Humboldt. This institute of learning can boast not only a number of famous teachers – including

The Humboldt University of Berlin.

Fichte, Hegel, Feuerbach, Schleiermacher and Schelling – but also many students who were to achieve international significance, for example, K. Marx, T. Mommsen, H. Helmholz, M. Planck, A. Einstein and the Brothers Grimm. In 1949, the former **Friedrich Wilhelm University** was renamed in honor of its founder, Wilhelm von Humboldt.

22 Neue Wache

Coming out of the University building, we turn left and continue along the north side of Unter den Linden for a couple of minutes until we reach the **Neue Wache**, which was built according to plans drawn up by Schinkel.

A further example of the classicism of Schinkel's style, this building was erected between 1816 and 1818 as the Royal Guardhouse (Königliche Wache). In 1931, Tessenow created here a monument in honor of the heroes and fallen of the First World War. After the last war, the Neue Wache underwent extensive rebuilding and, in 1960, a **Memorial for the Victims of Fascism and Militarism** was set up here. The Neue Wache now serves as the **Central Memorial of the Federal Republic of Germany**.

The Neue Wache is now the Central Memorial of the Federal Republic of Germany.

Just beyond the Neue Wache, we come to the **German Historical Museum** (Deutsches Historisches Museum) housed in the former arsenal (**Zeughaus**). This is one of the most important museums dealing with the history of Germany. The building, which has a square ground-plan and a 90-meter-long facade, was completed in 1706 and was the work of several architects, i.e., Nering, Schlüter, Grünberg and de Bodt. From 1730–1835, it was used to house the **Royal Armory**. After 1945, the damage incurred during the war was repaired and the building became the **Museum of German History** of the German Democratic Republic. Since 1990, it has been called the German Historical Museum.

German Historical Museum:
Unter den Linden 2, 10117 Berlin
Opening hours: Thurs.–Tues. 10 a.m. to 6 p.m.
Tel. 0 30–21 50 20

Courtgard of the German Historical Museum
in the former arsenal.

Continuing eastward along Unter den Linden, we soon come to the **Castle Bridge** (Schlossbrücke) over the River Spree, which leads us into the old city center of Berlin.

The bridge, which was based on drawings by K.F. Schinkel, was completed in 1824. With its richly ornamented railings and its marble sculptures, it is one of the most splendid bridges in the city.

The Castle Bridge with Berlin Cathedral in the background.

25 Lustgarten

Having crossed the bridge, we now see the extensive **Lustgarten** (Pleasure Garden) extending to our left.

On the commission of the "Great Elector," Frederick William, the Lustgarten was laid out on the site of the former Castle Garden (Schlossgarten) by Memhardt in 1650. Contemporary descriptions tell us that exotic ornamental plants once adorned this garden.

Immediately after his accession, Frederick I, the so-called "Soldier King," had the garden flattened and then converted into a military parade ground. Only in 1832 did Lenné and Schinkel restore the Lustgarten to its original function as a pleasure garden; however, about a century later, it was again – this time by the Nazis – turned into a parade ground. Although it ceased to have this function after the war, the actual form and layout of the Lustgarten have since remained fundamentally unchanged. The only surviving remnant of its previous history is the large granite bowl by C.G. Cantian that stands in front of the Old Museum. This was sculpted from a single block of stone before being highly polished.

26 Berlin Cathedral

To the east of the Lustgarten, we see the imposing, massive facade of **Berlin Cathedral** (Berliner Dom).

It was Kaiser William II who decided that the **Old Cathedral** (Alter Dom) – a more modest domed building with side wings – would have to make room for a new cathedral that would serve as the "main church of Prussian Protestantism in Berlin."

Famous for its role as the **burial place** of the Hohenzollerns, Berlin Cathedral was completed after many years of construction work in 1905.

View of Berlin Cathedral from the former Pleasure Garden (Lustgarten).

Based on plans by Raschdorff, its style is largely derived from the Italian High Renaissance, although its wealth of ornamentation as well as the numerous cupolas and towers result in a somewhat exaggeratedly pompous effect. The crypt contains a total of 95 tombs of members of the Hohenzollern family.

Work to repair the damage incurred by the church during the war was finally completed in 1982, so that the interior can now seat 1600 attending church services or one of the numerous concerts and other events frequently held here.

Berlin Cathedral by night.

7 Palace of the Republic

Crossing Unter den Linden once more, we come to the north side of the **Palace of the Republic** (Palast der Republik).

This enormous construction (180 meters long, 76 meters wide) was erected between 1973 and 1976 under the supervision of the architect, H. Graffunder. No building is so intimately linked with the history and times of the German Democratic Republic as the Palace of the Republic. Along with the assembly room of the People's Parliament (Volkskammer) sea ting up to 5000 people, this colossus covered with reflective glass also contains about 100 rooms, 13 restaurants and cafés, two discos, several galleries, a bowling alley and a theater.

Since it was opened in 1976, the Palace of the Republic can boast over 70 million visitors.

The Palace of the Republic on the Spree Canal.

28 Marx-Engels-Platz

The site now occupied by the square, **Marx-Engels-Platz**, and the Palace of the Republic was, until about 45 years ago, the location of **Hohenzollern Castle**, an immense building 200 meters long, 117 meters wide and (including its cupola) 70 meters high. Severely damaged by air attacks during the Second World War, it was completely demolished in 1950–51.

Crossing over to the west side of Marx-Engels-Platz, we come to the Foreign Ministry of the GDR located opposite on the other side of the Spree Canal. This huge modern construction was built by J. Kaiser between 1964 and 1967.

Marx-Engels-Platz can now claim to be the largest parking lot of downtown Berlin. Traditionally, it is the venue of the main **Berlin Christmas Market** as well as other events and celebrations.

9 Former Council of State Building

The southern part of Marx-Engels-Platz is dominated by the **Former Council of State Building** (ehemaliges Staatsratsgebäude).
Built from 1962 to 1964 under the supervision of H.E. Bogatzky and R. Korn, this was the permanent meeting place of the Council of State of the GDR until the merging of East and West Germany. The main entrance is a copy of the famous Eosander Portal that formerly adorned the now-demolished Hohenzollern Castle. The Eosander Portal had outstanding historical and symbolic significance for the GDR, as its balcony was the place from which Karl Liebknecht declared the "Free Socialist Republic" on 9th November, 1918.

0 Neuer Marstall

Passing along the front of the Former Council of State Building, we soon come to the **Neuer Marstall** (New Stables) located directly opposite the south side of the Palace of the Republic. Formerly a part of the south wing of Hohenzollern Castle, this building was erected between 1898 and 1900 on the basis of earlier plans by E. von Ihne. The building achieved its greatest celebrity on account of the so-called "red sailors" ("Rote Matrosen") who barricaded themselves in here during the 1918 revolution. The Neuer Marstall is now the main building of the **Berlin City Library** (Stadtbibliothek).

Nikolai Quarter

As we pass between the Palace of the Republic and the Neuer Marstall, we soon cross the River Spree over the so-called City Hall Bridge (Rathausbrücke) and then turn right into Poststrasse, which takes us into the **Nikolai Quarter** (Nikolaiviertel).
For the occasion of Berlin's 750th anniversary in 1987, this exact copy of the Old Nikolai Quarter was completed under the supervision of G. Stahn. Along with several original historic buildings and monuments that comprise this attractive quarter, we find in its center the oldest parish church in Berlin, the **Nikolai Church**, which dates from about 1230. This church was the venue, in 1539, of a ceremony marking the introduction of the Reformation into the Mark Brandenburg. Now a part of the **Märkisches Museum** dealing with the history of Brandenburg, the Nikolai Church is often used for exhibitions about Berlin's past.

The Nikolai Quarter, the original center of the city of Berlin.

2 Ephraim Palais

Following Poststrasse until it makes a sharp turn to the left, we come to the **Ephraim Palais**, standing on an elevation to our right.

This palais was built between 1761 and 1764 by F.W. Diterichs on the commission of Frederick II's court jeweler and banker. Owing to various traffic problems and road-widening schemes, the whole building was taken down in 1935; only between 1985 and 1987 were the 2493 individual parts of the building reassembled 20 meters away from the original site of the palais. The Ephraim Palais is now used by various museums as a place for exhibitions.

The Ephraim Palais and Nikolai Church.

3 Old City Hall

If we follow Poststrasse a little further, we soon come to the wide, busy street, the Mühlendamm, with the restaurant, Zur Rippe to our left. We turn left and go a short distance along Mühlendamm until we come to a large junction, where this street joins Spandauer-, Gruner- and Stralauer Strasse at the Molkenmarkt. Here, using the pedestrian crossing, we cross to Stralauer Strasse via the Molkenmarkt. This large square is dominated by the **Old City Hall** (Altes Stadthaus).

Constructed in 1911 as a building supplementary to the "Red City Hall" (Rotes Rathaus), this later served as the Seat of the Minister-Presidents of the GDR.

34 Parochial Church

Behind the Old City Hall, we leave Stralauer Strasse by turning left into Klosterstrasse. On the right, we see the so-called **Parochial Church**, the oldest Baroque ecclesiastical building in Berlin. It was built between 1695 and 1703 by M. Grünberg according to plans by J. A. Nering.

35 Zur Letzten Instanz – Berlin's Oldest Pub

Continuing for a few paces, we see on our left the medieval **City Mint** (Stadtmünze). At this junction, we leave Klosterstrasse and turn right into Parochialstrasse, which we follow right to the end where it joins Waisenstrasse. This brings us to the restaurant, **Zur letzten Instanz**.

The first mention of this inn dates back to about 1525, when it was referred to as a **"brandy bar"** (Brandweinstube). The many celebrities who have enjoyed a drink here include Napoleon, who supposedly sat on the ancient-looking fireside bench near the counter.

Here, one can enjoy many different Berlin specialities, including boiled knuckle of pork (Eisbein) with sauerkraut washed down with light Berliner Weisse beer (often served with a shot of fruit juice).

Berlin's oldest pub: once a "brandy bar", and now called Zur letzten Instanz.

6 Municipal Justice Building (Central Berlin)

Leaving Zur letzten Instanz, we turn right and continue along Waisen-strasse. We soon come to the last surviving remains of the **medieval city wall** from the thirteenth century. We now cross into Littenstrasse, which runs parallel with the ancient wall. This section is dominated by a build-ing in the Art Nouveau (Jugendstil) style, which houses the **Municipal Justice Authorities (Central Berlin)** (Stadtgericht Berlin-Mitte). Based on plans by P. Thoemer and R. Mönnich, this 220-meter-long building was constructed by O. Schmalz between 1896 and 1905. Of particular interest is the staircase located in the main entrance.

Remains of Berlin's medieval city wall dating from the thirteenth century.

7 Former Franciscan Monastery Church

Just before Littenstrasse takes us back to the noisy traffic of Gruner-strasse, we see on the left a small park, the path through which brings us to the **Franciscan Monastery Church**.

A Franciscan monastery was established on this site in 1249, resulting in the erection of this fine example of north-German Gothic brickwork architecture (Bæcksteingotik). Owing to severe damage suffered during bombing raids, this ruin had to be fenced off after the war, but the build-ing has now been secured and serves as a war memorial.

The former Franciscan Monastery Church.

38 "Red" City Hall

After a short walk, we come back to the large pedestrian crossing on the Molkenmarkt. Crossing this, we come to Spandauerstrasse, which we follow for a short distance before turning right into Rathausstrasse, where our attention is immediately drawn to the massive **"Red" City Hall** (Rotes Rathaus) directly in front of us.

Built on the foundation walls of the medieval City Hall, this enormous brick construction was erected between 1861 and 1869 by H.E. Waesemann on the basis of plans submitted during an international competition. This neo-Renaissance building complex has a surface area of 99 x 88 meters and a height of 74 meters, and comprises several wings enclosing three courtyards. Until the dissolution of the GDR, it served as the Seat of Government of the Lord Mayor as well as the meeting place of the City Council and Municipal Authorities of East Berlin. Since October 1991, it has been the home of the Senate of the City of Berlin.

The "Red" City Hall, the seat of government of the Lord Mayor of Berlin.

9 Church of St. Mary

Directly to the north of the City Hall, it's just a couple of hundred meters to the **Church of St. Mary** (Marienkirche).

Construction of this church began in about 1270, which makes it the second-oldest parish church of the city. St. Mary's was badly damaged during the city fire of 1370, but its reconstruction was completed soon after. The interior of the church contains much of interest, the most extraordinary feature being the "Dance of Death" (Totentanz) fresco, which is 2 meters high and 22.6 meters long, and was painted after the dreadful outbreak of plague in 1484. The bronze font dating from 1437 and the Baroque marble pulpit (1703) by A. Schlüter are also outstanding. Close by the church door, we see a "cross of atonement" (Sühnekreuz), which recalls the violent end of Provost Nicolaus von Bernau in 1325, who fell foul of the citizens' anti-clerical sentiments toward the Roman clergy.

The Church of St. Mary on Karl-Liebknecht-Strasse.

40 Berlin Television Tower

Finding the **Television Tower** (Fernsehturm) should not be a problem, as it is not only the tallest building in Berlin but, with a height of 365 meters, the second-largest building in Europe. Based on an idea of H. Henselmann and designs by the architects, F. Dieter and G. Franke, the tower began operation on 3rd October 1969.

At their respective heights of 203 and 207 meters, the viewing platform and Tele-Café offer visitors (weather permitting) marvelous views of the city extending to a distance of 40 kilometers. At the base of the tower (which weighs 26.000 tonnes), there is an exhibition centre with frequent changes of program.

Berlin Television Tower:
Panoramastrasse 1a, 10178 Berlin
Opening hours: Daily 9 a.m. to 12 p.m.
(last admission, 11 p.m.) / Tel. 030–5348080

With a height of 365 meters, Berlin's Television Tower is the second-largest building in Europe. ▶

Although, strictly speaking, **Alexanderplatz** actually includes the area in front of the entrance of the Television Tower, it is generally considered that the "real" Alexanderplatz is the large square located on the other side of the streetcar station.

The former **Ochsenplatz** – once a parade ground and market place located outside the gates of the city – was given its present name in memory of Tsar Alexander I, who visited Berlin in 1805.

During the war, this square was virtually reduced to a heap of rubble. The fact that its subways and undergound passages were of strategic impor-

Alexanderplatz with the Berolinahaus and the Kaufhaus.

tance for the Nazi defense of the city meant that it was a frequent target of Allied bomb attacks.

Thus, after 1945, Alexanderplatz was transformed from the city's largest traffic junction into the most spacious pedestrian precinct in Berlin. Only two existing buildings – the **Berolinahaus** and the **Alexanderhaus** – were able to be incorporated into the completely new layout of the square. The new buildings that were eventually added include the Forum Hotel constructed in 1967–70 (the work of an "architect's collective"), the Kaufhaus on the north side of the square built at the same time, the famous **World Time Clock** (Weltzeituhr; 1969) designed by the artist and architect, E. John, and the centrally placed **Fountain of Friendship of the Nations** (Brunnen der Völkerfreundschaft; 1969) by the artist, W. Womacka. Among the other buildings around Alexanderplatz, the most striking are the **"Teacher's House"** (Haus des Lehrers) to the east with its colorful frieze, and the **Congress Hall** (Kongresshalle) with its shallow dome. As nowadays, Alexanderplatz was considered to be the focal point and center of the capital of the GDR and was thus the venue of many important events and celebrations.

The World Time Clock, a favorite stopping point for visitors to Berlin.

Walking Tour of West Berlin

Those now wishing to continue their tour into the west part of the city should proceed to Karl-Liebknecht-Strasse which runs along the north side of Alexanderplatz. Directly opposite the streetcar (S-Bahn) station Alexanderplatz, there is a bus stop for bus no. 100, which runs every 10 minutes. Taking this, it is only five stops to the starting point of our tour of West Berlin the Reichstag building.

12 Reichstag Building

A grandiose piece of Wilhelmine architecture in the style of the Italian High Renaissance, the **Reichstag** was built between 1884 and 1894 according to plans by P. Wallot. As so many buildings of this period, the Reichstag was meant to reflect the might and power of the recently established German state. It was the place of assembly of the parliaments of the German Empire until 1918, before being used as the seat of government of the Weimar Republic and, after 1933, the Third Reich. When the government of Germany is transferred to Berlin, it will be the meeting place of the Bundestag.

It was from the imposing main entrance of the Reichstag that P. Scheide-mann declared the German Republic on 9th November, 1918. Fifteen years later – in the night of 27th February, 1933 – the interior of the building was largely gutted as a result of the Reichstag Fire. This deliberate act of vandalism by the Nazis under the immediate supervision of Göring provided the Fascists with an excuse to launch a wave of mass arrests of political sympathizers of the Left. On 30th April, 1945, Soviet soldiers celebrated the victory over Hitler's Third Reich by displaying the Red Flag on the Reichstag building.

The Reichstag Building.

43 House of the Cultures of the World

Taking the bus no. 100 again, it's only two stops to the **House of the Cultures of the World** (Haus der Kulturen der Welt; formerly, the Kongresshalle).

This was built in 1957 according to plans of the American architect, A. Stubbins, as part of the so-called Interbau project. The square platform rests on foundations composed of nearly 1000 concrete posts. The large, central auditorium seats 1250 persons; along with numerous smaller conference rooms, the House of the Cultures of the World contains an exhibition hall and a restaurant. As its name indicates, this building is dedicated to the various cultures of the world, serving as the venue of large-scale exhibitions and international congresses.

House of the Cultures of the World:
John-Foster-Dulles-Allee 10,
10557 Berlin
Tel. 0 30 – 39 78 70

44 Bellevue Castle

Our next destination is also best reached by taking bus no. 100: just one stop from the House of the Cultures of the World, we come **Bellevue Castle** (Schloss Bellevue).

Bellevue Castle, the permanent residence of the President of Germany.

This early classical palace in the French Baroque style was built during the reign of Frederick II in 1785 according to plans by Boumann. After being severely damaged during the war, Bellevue Castle was restored to ts former splendor in 1959. The **Castle Garden** has an area of about 20 hectares. Bellevue Castle is now the permanent residence of the President of Germany.

45 Victory Column

Following Spreeweg roughly southward from Bellevue Castle, it's only about 150 meters to the large traffic roundabout, the so-called "Great Star" (Grosser Stern).

Rising from the center of this star-shaped junction, we see the **Victory Column** (Siegessäule), which is almost 60 meters high and crowned by a gilded figure representing "Victoria." This imposing monument was erected to commemorate the various wars fought by Prussia that resulted in the Unification of Germany. Incorporating a number of "spoils of war," the column was commissioned by Kaiser William I and was completed in 1873 using designs by J. H. Strack.

Each year, about 150.000 visitors climb the 285 steps that lead up through the inside of the column to the viewing platform that offers fine views of the nearby park, the Tiergarten.

The Victory Column on the "Great Star" junction.

The Victory Column is entirely surrounded by a vast park, the **Berlin Tiergarten**. This landscaped park designed by Lenné (1833–1847) was completely destroyed. After 1945, numerous projects led to the planting of thousands of trees and shrubs, so that one of the most popular parks in the city is again a joy to visit. Criss-crossed by winding paths, the Tiergarten contains a pleasing mixture of open fields, woodland and lakes, amid which there are numerous monuments to important figures in the history of German culture. In addition to the composers' memorial to Haydn, Beethoven and Mozart we also find memorials to great authors such as J. W. v. Goethe and E. Lessing.

At the east end of the Tiergarten – not far from the Brandenburg Gate – we find the **Soviet Memorial** (Sowjetisches Ehrenmal), which commemorates the Soviet soldiers that lost their lives during the liberation of Berlin. Flanked by two tanks that were actually used during the capture of the city, the monument has the form of a broad, marble portal surmounted by a bronze statue of a Soviet soldier.

47 Memorial of German Resistance

Taking the Grosse Stern junction as our starting point, we take the large path (Grosser Weg) through the south-east section of the Tiergarten (this takes a diagonal course between the Strasse des 17. Juli and the Hofjäger-allee). We continue on this path through the park until we come to Tiergartenstrasse. After we have crossed Tiergartenstrasse, we finally come to Stauffenbergstrasse, where we find the **Memorial of German Resistance** (Gedenkstätte Deutscher Widerstand).

The Memorial of German Resistance.

The complex of buildings was built from 1911 to 1914 under the direction of the architects Süssmuth and Reinhardt to serve as the administrative building for the **German Ministry of the Navy**. In 1938 it became the headquarters of the **Supreme Army Command.**

Ten years after the seizure of power by the Nazis, the assassination plot against Hitler and Lieutenant Claus Schenk Graf von Stauffenberg failed. As a result, in the night of the 20th to 21st July 1944 five officers were executed by shooting in the inner courtyard (now the court of honor) of the "Bendlerblock."

On the second storey there is now a permanent exhibition commemorating the group led by Stauffenberg and numerous other groups which resisted nationalism.

Memorial of German Resistance:
Stauffenbergstrasse 13–14, 10557 Berlin
Opening hours: Mon.-Fri. 9 a.m. to 6 p.m., Sat./Sun. 9 a.m.
to 1 p.m. / Tel. 0 30–26 54 22 02

48 Philharmonie

After returning a short distance along Stauffenbergstrasse, we turn right into Sigismundstrasse and then left into Matthäikirchstrasse, which soon brings us to a remarkable modern building, the **Berlin Philharmonie**.

The Philharmonie.

Situated just to the south of the Tiergarten, this was built according to plans drawn up by H. Scharoun between 1960 and 1963. With its generous dimensions and gleaming gold-colored facade, this marvelous construction embodies a fascinating combination of architectonic forms centered on a large concert hall, whose terrace-form seating arrangement provides room for an audience of 2200.

Philharmonie:
Matthäikirchstrasse 1,
10785 Berlin
Tel. 0 30–25 48 80

State Library of Berlin – Prussian Cultural Trust, House II in Potsdamer Strasse.

19 State Library of Berlin – Prussian Cultural Trust, House II

Following Margaretenstrasse (to the south of the Philharmonie), we soon come to the massive **State Library of Berlin – Prussian Cultural Trust, House II** (Staatsbibliothek II) located on Potsdamer Strasse.
One of the biggest library buildings in Europe, its architectural style has much in common with that of the Philharmonie. Like the latter, it is the work of H. Scharoun, who supervised the construction of this "palace of books" until its completion in 1978. The enormous reading rooms of this library offer seating for up to 600 visitors.

50 New National Gallery

Almost directly opposite the State Library on the other side of Potsdamer Strasse, we see the modern **New National Gallery**. Built in 1968 as a counterpart to the National Gallery in East Berlin, this is a prime example of the "doubling" of city buildings that occurred during the separation of East and West Berlin.

The New National Gallery.

This noteworthy construction was designed by Mies van der Rohes, who employed a minimal range of building materials (steel and glass) to achieve a remarkably impressive work of architecture.
The New National Gallery shows the art of the 20th century (from Edvard Munch to Barnett Newman).

51 Bauhaus Archive

We continue along the Reichspietsch Ufer, a street running along the Landwehr Canal to the south of the New National Gallery. From the bus stop here, we take the bus no. 129 as far as Van der Heydt/Ecke Klingel-höferstrasse (three stops away). On the left, we now see the **Bauhaus Archive**.

The great architect, Walter Gropius, drew up the plans and designs for this building, which was only actually constructed in 1979, 10 years after his death.

The aesthetic style, the bright colors and the emphatic forms that are so striking in this museum building are characteristic features of Gropius' architectural oeuvre.

Among the many works on display in the Bauhaus Archive, the architectural models as well as the collection of "design furniture" are of particular interest. From these, it becomes clear just what a significant influence the Bauhaus movement has exerted, and continues to exert, on the development of modern industrial design.

52 Zoological Garden/Aquarium

Leaving the Bauhaus, we cross the canal to reach Lützowplatz and, from here, take the bus no. 100. Just one stop away, we come to the "Elephant Gate", the main entrance to the **Zoological Garden** in Budapester Strasse.

The Zoological Garden has occupied its present site since the last century, its establishment being largely the work of M.H. Lichtenstein and A. von Humboldt with the assistance of the landscape gardener, P.J. Lenné.

Spread over an area of 35 hectares, the Zoological Garden is home to at least 14.000 animals belonging to about 1500 different species.

To the west of the Zoo, we find the railway station, the **Bahnhof Zoologischer Garten**, which was completed in 1936, and is now one of the most important traffic junctions in the city. The site of the Zoological Garden extends east from here as far as the Landwehr Canal.

The famous **Berlin Aquarium** is to be found just to the right of the Elephant Gate, which dates back to 1899.

First established in 1869 by the renowned zoologist, Alfred Brehm, the Aquarium was situated in Unter den Linden (on the corner of Schadowstrasse) until 1910. Three years later, it was transferred to the site of the Zoological Garden. The more than 700 different species on show embrace fishes, reptiles, snails and insects from all over the world. Each year, the Zoo and Aquarium welcome about 3 million visitors.

Zoological Garden / Aquarium:
Budapester Strasse,
10789 Berlin
Opening hours: Daily 9 a.m. to 6 p.m.

The "Elephant Gate", the main entrance to the Zoological Garden.

53 Europa Center

Continuing from the Elephant Gate, we leave Budapester Strasse to our right to arrive at Breitscheidtplatz. With a height of 86 meters, the **Europa Center** – built between 1963 and 1965 from plans by H. Hentrich and H. Petschnigg – immediately arrests our attention.

In addition to containing several cinemas, this building chiefly serves as business premises and as a shopping center. Several insurance companies and joint-stock companies have their headquarters here, but the main point of interest for visitors is the wide range of shops, restaurants and cafés that are to be found in the first two storeys.

In addition to a casino, the satirical cabaret revue, **"Die Stachel-schweine"** ("The Porcupines") has its home in the basement storey of the Europa Center.

The 13-meter-high 'water-clock' in the Europa Center.

The construction of the **Globe Fountain** (Weltkugelbrunnen) on Breitscheidplatz in 1983 finally put an end to the heavy traffic around the Europa Center. A work by the sculptor, J. Schmettau, the fountain is meant to depict the world political situation in the year of its construction. The Globe Fountain, like the World Time Clock on Alexanderplatz, enjoys the reputation of being one of the most popular meeting places in the city.

The Globe Fountain next to the Europa Center.

55 | Kaiser William Church of Remembrance

The focal point of Breitscheidplatz and the best-known symbol of West Berlin is the **Church of Remembrance** (Gedächtniskirche). Built in 1891–95 in the neo-Romanesque style according to plans by the architect, F. Schwechten, the church received severe damage as the result of a direct hit during a bombing raid on 22nd November, 1943.

After the war, it was decided to retain the surviving section as a ruin and incorporate the 63-meter-high tower into a new construction. The new tower, which is 53 meters tall, is made of glazed concrete blocks and contains six bells. The ruined tower and modern chapel are linked by a passage. Each full hour, there is a carillon of bells in the old tower.

The partially ruined Kaiser William Church of Remembrance with its modern church building.

Starting at Breidscheidplatz and extending westward, the **Kurfürstendamm** is one of Berlin's most famous streets. This boulevard was given its present layout in 1883, before which it was merely a rather modest bridlepath. Looking at the many splendid buildings from the turn of the century that have been carefully restored to their original condition, it is easy to see why, even before the war, the Kurfürstendamm was one of the most

Café Kranzler on the Kurfürstendamm.

exclusive and expensive areas in the west part of Berlin. A stroll down this kilometer-long street takes us past any number of restaurants, cafés and tempting shops and boutiques, not to mention several famous places – for example, **Café Kranzler** and the luxurious **Hotel Kempinski** – whose names are firmly established among the "must-sees" of tourist Berlin.

7 Käthe Kollwitz Museum

From the Kurfürstendamm just past the **Ku 'damm Eck**, we take the next left turn into Joachimstaler Strasse. After a short distance, we turn right into Lietzenburger Strasse and then take the second street to the right, Fasanenstrasse.

House number 24 in this street is a late-classical building that contains a museum devoted to the sculpture and drawings of the artist, **Käthe Kollwitz**. The sufferings of the poor and the working classes as well as the passionate condemnation of war were the dominant themes and political motivation of this artist's powerful oeuvre (cycles of graphic works: Memorial for the Fallen; the Weavers' Revolt; the Peasants' War).

The Museum contains a collection of 100 prints, 70 drawings and original plates as well as numerous sculptures by Käthe Kollwitz.

Käthe Kollwitz Museum:
Fasanenstrasse 24, 10719 Berlin
Opening hours: Weds.–Mon. 11 a.m. to 6 p.m.
Tel. 030–8825210

Information

---

8 Jewish Community House

Passing the so-called **Literaturcafé**, we soon cross the Kurfürstendamm and continue along Fasanenstrasse on the other side.

The old **synagogue** that once stood here was built by E. Hessel in 1911/12 but was burned down by the Nazis on 9th November, 1938. Of what remained of this building, only the entrance portal was able to be integrated into the new **Jewish Community House** (Jüdisches Gemeindehaus) that was constructed by H. Heise and D. Knoblauch in 1957–59.

In the columned courtyard of this building, there is a memorial erected in memory of the countless Jews of Berlin who were murdered by the Nazis. The Jewish Community House is the central meeting place of those citizens of Berlin who adhere to the Jewish faith.

---

9 Theater of the West

Continuing northward along Fasanenstrasse, we eventually come to Kantstrasse; here, on the opposite side of the road, we see the **Theater of the West** (Theater des Westens).

Designed by B. Sehring and built in 1895/96, it is a good example of the architectural style termed "Wilhelmine historicism." Although the program of this theater is largely devoted to modern musicals, it has also been the venue of productions of classical operettas in recent years.

Theater of the West:
Kantstrasse 12,
10623 Berlin
Tel. 0 30–3 19 03; Fax 0 30–31 90 31 88

60 College of the Arts

Following Kantstrasse to the left, we take the next turning on the right into Uhlandstrasse. Walking along this street, we see many buildings that give us an idea of the domestic architecture favored by the well-to-do in old Berlin. Reaching the end of Uhlandstrasse, we arrive at Steinplatz, where opposite us in Hardenbergstrasse, the imposing building of the **College of the Arts** (Hochschule der Künste) dominates the scene.

A good example of the Wilhelmine neo-Baroque style, this was completed in 1902 in accordance with plans by H. Kayser and K. von Grossheim. Since 1975, this building has served as the College of the Arts, unifying under one roof the College of Fine Art and the College of Music and the Performing Arts.

61 Ernst-Reuter-Platz

Following Hardenbergstrasse in a westerly direction, it's about 300 meters until we reach – after passing the Goethe Institut – **Ernst-Reuter-Platz**.

Measuring 130 x 117 meters, this is one of the biggest city squares in Europe. Five major streets converge into the traffic roundabout that surrounds it. The center of the square contains lawns and flower beds, along with 41 fountains in two large pools. Several of the modern buildings grouped around the square belong to the **Technological University of Berlin**.

The square was named after Ernst Reuter, the first Lord Mayor of West Berlin, in 1953.

62 Schiller Theater

Bismarckstrasse runs into the west side of Ernst-Reuter-Platz, and it is at the beginning of this street that we come to the **Schiller Theater**.

This theater was built in 1905–07 according to plans drawn up by M. Littmann and J. Heilmann. Despite war damage, its exterior has remained largely unchanged, although the interior has undergone several major renovations and alterations. Since its controversial closure as a drama theater on 1st January 1996, the traditional **Schiller Theater** has been a private musical theater.

Schiller Theater:
Bismarckstrasse 110
10625 Berlin
Tel. 0 30–31 11 31 00, Fax 0 30–31 11 32 00

3 German Opera Berlin

We continue westward along Bismarckstrasse until we see the large modern building of the **German Opera Berlin** (Deutsche Oper Berlin) on the right.

Owing to severe war damage, it was not feasible to reconstruct the original opera house that stood on this site
(designed by H. von Sehling and completed in 1912). Thus, a completely new building for the German Opera was designed by Börnemann and opened in 1961. This highly regarded opera house offers seating for an audience of 1885 persons.

The German Opera Berlin.

Continuing westward along Bismarckstrasse, it's about 500 meters until we reach Kaiser-Friedrich-Strasse, the third turning on the right. From here we take bus no. 109 (direction, Flughafen Tegel) as far as the stop on Luisenplatz.

We now come to one of the city's finest Rococo buildings, **Charlottenburg Castle**, with its delightful garden, the **Schlosspark**. The construction of this castle began in 1695 on the commission of the king, who wished it to serve as a summer palace for the queen, Sophie Charlotte. The central section was based on designs by J. A. Nehring, and other parts were gradually added, including the large courtyard, the Ehrenhof, the 48-meter-high domed tower, the orangerie, the Knobelsdorff Wing and, finally, the theater. As a result of these additions, the castle eventually attained an imposing length of about 500 meters.

The exterior and interior of the castle underwent painstaking restoration after the Second World War. This involved not only restoring the castle's original color scheme but also the application of the same building and decoration techiques as those used at the time of its construction. The most noteworthy examples that illustrate the authenticity of the restoration work are the two main halls (Festsäle), which Knobelsdorff decorated in the most ornate Rococo style, and the large dining hall (Grosser Speisesaal) with its pink marbled-stucco decoration and molding. Inside the castle, there are excellent collections of paintings and porcelain as well as a **Museum of Prehistory and Early History** (Museum für Vor- und Frühgeschichte). Containing a wealth of exhibits ranging in date from

Charlottenburg Castle.

5000 B.C. to about 1500 A.D., this museum provides fascinating insights into the early history of Europe and the Orient.

The garden that extends behind the castle, the Schlosspark, is one of the largest parks in Berlin.

Laid out in 1697 in the French style by Siméon, this garden was – largely through the efforts of Lenné – transformed into an "English garden" at the turn of the nineteenth century. Located by the east entrance of the garden, the new pavilion was designed by Schinkel and built in 1824/25. The 24 marble busts of Roman emperors and their wives date from 1663 and provide impressive evidence of the artistic skills of the period.

Whereas access to the garden was, at first, confined to a few privileged persons, its gates are now open to all. With its expansive areas of woodland and lawns as well as its beautiful lakes, it is hardly surprising that, in summer, this garden is one of the most popular places of relaxation for those who live in Berlin.

Charlottenburg Castle:
Spandauer Damm, 14059 Berlin
Opening hours: Tues.–Fri. 9 a.m. to 5 p.m.,
Sat./Sun. 10 a.m. to 5 p.m., Tel. 030–32091–1

5 Egyptian Museum

Leaving the castle through the main gate, we cross the Spandauer Damm and then enter Schloss-Strasse directly opposite. Here, on the left, we come to the **Egyptian Museum** (Ägyptisches Museum).

The building that has served as the home of this museum since 1967 was originally a guards' barracks (**Gardekaserne**) and was built between 1851 and 1859 by Stüler.

The most famous exhibit in the museum's collection is the bust of **"Queen Nefertiti"**, a work of the 18th Dynasty dating from about 1340 B.C. However, this is only one of the many superb works on show, which include the remarkable **Lion's Head of Niuserre** from 2450 B.C., the finest of the numerous animal sculptures of the collection. Another work of outstanding interest is the picture of a young royal couple, "The Walk in the Garden," dating from 2400 B.C.

Taken together, the exhibits in the museum provide a broad survey of main epochs of Egyptian civilization.

Egyptian Museum:
Schloss-Strasse 70, 14059 Berlin
Opening hours: Tues.–Fri. 9 a.m. to 5 p.m.; Sat./Sun. 10 a.m. to 5 p.m., Mon. closed, Tel. 030–32091261

Egyptian Museum: Nefertiti.

66 Bröhan Museum

Next to the Museum of Classical Art, we find the **Bröhan Museum**, which was opened in 1983 on the ground floor of a building that formerly served as an infantry barracks. This extensive collection was donated to the city of Berlin by Karl H. Bröhan in 1982.

The museum contains almost 1600 exhibits, including porcelain, glass, paintings and sculptures, as well as exquisite Art Nouveau (Jugendstil) furniture dating from the period 1890–1940.

7 Broadcasting House

Continuing southward along Schloss-Strasse, it's about 400 meters to the subway (U-Bahn) station, Sophie-Charlotte-Platz. Taking the subway in the direction, Ruhleben, it's just two stops until we reach Theodor-Heuss-Platz.

In the large avenue, Masurenallee, which leads roughly north-eastward from this square, the dominant building is **Broadcasting House** (Haus des Rundfunks), which was built between 1929 and 1931, and was Germany's first broadcasting center. After the war between 1945 and 1956, the building was under the control of the Soviet occupation forces. During this period, it was the transmission center of the East Berlin radio station, **Ost-Berliner Rundfunk**. The main studio and radio department of the SFB are now located in Broadcasting House.

Broadcasting House seen from the Radio Tower.

68 Exhibition Center and International Congress Center (ICC)

Just to the east of Theodor-Heuss-Platz on the site of the nearby **Exhibition Center** (Messegelände), we see the **International Congress Center** (ICC).

This monumental building was completed on 2nd April, 1979, after 9 years of construction work. Being 320 meters long, 80 meters wide and 40 meters high, it is one of the largest building complexes in Berlin. Owing to its outer covering composed of several layers and its heavy steel roof weighing 8500 tons, this remarkable silver-colored construction is completely isolated from traffic noise and external vibration. The largest hall in the ICC has a seating capacity of 5000, and the building contains eight smaller halls as well as 80 conference rooms and an auditorium with stage equipped with the latest technical refinements. Thus, the excellent facilities and the organizational framework offered by the ICC makes it the ideal venue for large-scale conferences and events. The ICC is linked by a modern multistorey bridge to the exhibition halls of the nearby Exhibition Center. Each year, the ICC plays host to about 400,000 participants from all over the world attending international trade fairs and congresses.

69 Radio Tower and German Broadcasting Museum

Close to the Exhibition Center, the **Berlin Radio Tower** (Funkturm) rises to a height of 150 meters. The tower's viewing platform and restaurant can be reached by means of an elevator.

The Radio Tower was built in 1924 according to plans of Heinrich Straumer and went into operation 2 years later on the occasion of the third German **Funkausstellung** (Radio Exhibition). As well as offering lovely views of the city, it also provides interesting insights into the history of broadcasting in Germany. Since 1967, the **German Broadcasting Museum** (Deutsches Rundfunkmuseum) has been housed in a former studio located just at the base of the Radio Tower. The exhibition here covers all of the important stages in the development of radio technology in the period 1923–33 and includes a complete reconstruction of the first German radio studio dating from 1923.

Information

Radio Tower: Messedamm 11, 14055 Berlin
Opening hours: Daily 10 a.m. to 9:30 p.m.,
Tel. 030–3038 2996
German Broadcasting Museum:
Hammerskjöldplatz 1, 14055 Berlin
Opening hours: Weds.–Mon. 10 a.m. to 5 p.m.
Tel. 030–3028186

Returning to Theodor-Heuss-Platz, we continue our tour by taking the subway train no. 2 to the **Olympic Stadium** (Olympiastadion), which is just two stops away. The stadium itself lies to the west of the subway station and takes about 10 minutes to reach on foot.

The Olympic Stadium was built by Albert Speer on the orders of Hitler between 1934 and 1936 using revised plans drawn up by the brothers, Werner and Walter March. Its monumental dimensions were intended "to document the invincible power of Germany." The symmetric-axial form of construction as well as the pseudo-sacred character of the building seem to reflect the megalomania of its creators.

In the summer of 1936 – a time when the first Berlin Jews were being deported to concentration camps – it was here that Hitler opened the **Olympic Games**, which he cynically exploited as a massive international propaganda exercise on behalf of the Third Reich.

The Olympia Stadium has room for about 90,000 spectators and is now used for football matches, large sporting events and rock concerts. The site also includes an **hockey** and **horse-riding stadium**, as well as the **swimming hall** located to the north.

The Olympic Stadium.

Kaufhaus des Westens (KaDeWe)

Returning to the Olympiastadion subway station, we now take the eastward-bound train no. 2 until we reach Wittenbergplatz, which is nine stops away. Here, at the junction of Tauentzienstrasse, Passauerstrasse and Ansbacherstrasse, we come to the largest department store in Europe, the **Kaufhaus des Westens** (for short, KaDeWe). With a sales area of about 43.000 square-meters, this veritable emporium attracts 80,000 customers each day with its formidable array of wares. The food department alone offers a seemingly infinite range of international specialities, all of them as fresh and beautifully presented as one could wish to see.

The building was constructed for the retail magnate, A. Jandorf, by the architect, J.E. Schaudt, in 1906/07, but was taken over in 1927 by the famous department-store entrepreneur, Hermann Tietz (Hertie).

KaDeWe:
Tauentzienstrasse 21–24
10772 Berlin
Tel. 030–21210

72 Urania

Close to Wittenbergplatz at the corner of Kleiststrasse and An der Urania is the **Urania**, a venue for scientific and academic lectures. The Urania Society was founded in 1888 by the scientists W. Vogel and W. v. Siemens. It was the center of a vigorous expansion of scientific adult education. In 1954 the Urania was constituted as an association, which today has about 6000 members. The Urania devotes itself to making scientific knowledge available to the lay person, with excellent lectures in all fields of knowledge. The Urania is also Berlin's largest program cinema and the site of theater and concert performances and regular exhibitions.

Urania:
An der Urania 17
10787 Berlin
Tel. 030–2189091

73 Anhalt Railway Station

From the subway station on Wittelsbachplatz, we now take a bus no. 129 in the direction, Hermannsplatz, and get off at the streetcar station, Anhalter Bahnhof.

From here, we can see the remains of the **Anhalt Railway Station**, which was built in the Renaissance style by F. Schwechten between 1874 and 1880. The station is located on Askanischer Platz, which has a firm place in history, as it was the point of departure of A. Borsig's first steam locomotive in 1841, which traveled as far as Jüterbog. The "Anhalter," as the people of Berlin called it, was one of the four major railway stations that were once the focus of the city's incoming and outgoing passenger traffic.

Severe war damage ruled out further use of this station after the mid-1950s, so that, with the exception of the main entrance, the building was completely demolished.

However, even as a ruin, the Anhalt Railway Station is still attractive and worth seeing, as is shown by the number of visitors that still include it in a sight-seeing tour.

Remains of the former Anhalt Railway Station.

4 Martin Gropius Building

If we now proceed roughly northward along Stresemannstrasse, we see – on the right set back from the street – a large Renaissance-style building, which was constructed by Martin Gropius in 1881.

Although badly damaged in the war, the **Martin Gropius Building** has, in the past years, been largely restored to its original condition.

Along with being the venue of changing exhibitions, this building houses the **Berlin Gallery** (Berlinische Galerie), which is concerned with the art and cultural history of the city of Berlin.

To the east of the Martin Gropius Building in the former Prinz-Albrecht-Strasse, we can find the remains of the building that, between 1933 and 1945, served as the headquarters of the the dreaded State Secret Police (Gestapo) as well as the operational headquarters of the head of the SS and mass-murderer, Heinrich Himmler. Today, it is still possible to see the cellar in which countless opponents of the Fascist regime were tortured and murdered. The site is now a "documentation and memorial place" ("Dokumentations- und Gedächtnisstätte").

Martin Gropius Building:
Stresemannstrasse 110
10963 Berlin
Opening hours: Tues.–Sun. 10 a.m. to 8 p.m.

The Martin Gropius Building, the venue of mony interesting exhibitions.

75 Former Checkpoint Charlie

Just behind the site of the Martin Gropius Building, we come to Wilhelmstrasse, which we now cross in order to reach Kochstrasse.

Not far from the point at which Kochstrasse joins Wilhelmstrasse, we come to the former **border crossing** controlled by the Allied forces until 1990.

The border clossing, **Checkpoint Charlie**, became world-famous when, in 1961, it was the scene of a dramatic East-West confrontation. As the tension of the Cold War reached its peak, Soviet and American tanks with lowered guns took up position on either side of the checkpoint, a potentially explosive situation of international dimensions that was finally defused after diplomatic negotiations. Located a short distance from the former border crossing, the **Haus am Checkpoint Charlie** contains a fascinating collection of devices – including specially converted cars, home-made small aircraft and motorized kites – which ingenious East German citizens used to effect their escape from the DDR.

Haus am Checkpoint Charlie:
Friedrichstrasse 44, 10969 Berlin
Opening hours: Daily 9 a.m. to 10 p.m.
Tel. 030–2511031

Information

The Haus am Checkpoint Charlie.

6 Berlin Museum

Proceeding eastward along Kochstrasse, we take the second turning on the right into Markgrafenstrasse and continue along this street until it joins Lindenstrasse. On the opposite side of the road, we now see the **Berlin Museum**.

The museum was established in this three-winged Baroque building, the former **Supreme Court Building** (Kammergerichtsgebäude), in 1968. Constructed in 1734/35 under the supervision of P. Gerlach, it was designed to accomodate various administrative authorities and legal departments that had previously been housed in the royal castle.

The extensive collection of the museum comprises exhibits documenting the history of the city of Berlin and its culture. Along with drawings by the famous Berlin artist, Heinrich Zille, there are also many articles – ranging from toys to furniture – reflecting everyday life and life styles during various periods in Berlin. Many of the pieces on show date back over 300 years.

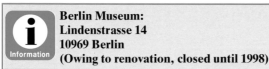

i Information

Berlin Museum:
Lindenstrasse 14
10969 Berlin
(Owing to renovation, closed until 1998)

We now return to the Anhalt Railway Station and, from there, take a bus no. 248 (direction, Büdnerring) back to the Reichstag building, the starting point of our tour of West Berlin.

Excursions in and around Berlin

77 Wannsee

Located on the south-west outskirts of Berlin, the attractive lake, the **Wannsee**, can easily be reached by streetcar from the city center.

For some, the Wannsee means a suburb with lovely old villas, while for others, it's a favorite place for leisure and relaxation.

Berlin's "Lido," the so-called Strandbad Wannsee, was first opened to the public in 1907. The sand "beach" is about 1 mile long and about 80 meters wide. The delightful surroundings of the lake are considered to be a paradise for water sports and leisure activities. As well as offering swimming and sailing facilities, the lake has a popular restaurant, **"Die Wannseeterrassen,"** which is an ideal place for a relaxing meal. Close to the Wannsee streetcar station, there is a jetty from which it is possible to take an enjoyable boat ride on one of the lake's many pleasure steamers.

On the west bank of the Wannsee, in the street "Am Grossen Wannsee", the villa at number 56–58 was the site of the so-called Wannsee Conference of 20th January 1942, where details of the program of extermination of European Jews, which had already begun, were discussed. Since 1992 this has been the site of a memorial and education center. Three kilometers south-west of here, by the smaller lake, the Kleiner Wannsee, is the grave of the author, **Heinrich von Kleist**. On 21st November, 1811, he and Henriette Vogel committed suicide near the small Wannsee Bridge.

8 Treptower Park

Located close to the River Spree in the east part of Berlin, **Treptower Park** extends over an area of 53 hectares. Close to the streetcar station, Treptower Park, there is a jetty for ships of the so-called "White Fleet" (Weisse Flotte), whose program of boat rides includes "coffee trips" through the waterways of the city.

The famous **Archenhold Observatory** (Sternwarte) is situated in the south-east section of this park. Founded by the astronomer, Friedrich Simon, this was built in 1896 on the occasion of the Berlin Trade Fair (Berliner Gewerbeaustellung). The observatory contains a gigantic, 21-meter-telescope, which can be seen during a guided tour.

In the lovely section of the park to the west of the observatory, there is the largest and most important monument to the Soviet soldiers that lost their lives during the liberation of Berlin. This Memorial was erected between 1947 and 1949 according to plans drawn up by J. V. Wutschetitsch, S. S. Walerius and J. B. Belopolski. Close to the entrance portal in the forecourt of the central section of the monument, there is a figure symbolizing the mourning "Motherland" (Mutter Heimat) sculpted from a single block of granite. The "Field of Honor" (Ehrenhain), on both sides of which stand eight stone sarcophagi, is the final resting place of 5000 Soviet soldiers. The central point of the memorial comprises a hill surmounted by a mausoleum and a massive figure (11.6 meters high) of a Soviet soldier, whose left arm holds a child while he smashes a swastika with the sword in his right hand.

9 Müggelsee and Müggelberge

Located in the south-east of the city and best reached via the streetcar station, Köpenick, the lake, **Müggelsee** and the nearby hills, the **Müggelberge**, represent one of the largest and most picturesque leisure areas of Berlin. With a surface area of 7.46 square-kilometers, the Müggelsee is ideal for sailing, water-skiing and, of course, swimming. Along with many large "beaches," the lake also offers smaller, secluded places for sunbathing and swimming. To the south between the Müggelsee and the smaller lake, the **Teufelssee**, lie the wooded hills, the Müggelberge, which rise to a height of 115 meters and are thus the highest natural elevations in the city and its surrounding area. Situated at a height of about 90 meters between hills and dense woodland, the 30-meter-high **Müggel Tower** has a viewing platform as well as containing a restaurant. The Müggelberge, whose terrain includes moorland, are the home of a broad spectrum of flora and fauna.

Müggel Tower:
In den Müggelbergen, 12559 Berlin
Opening hours: Mon.–Fri. 10 a.m. to 7 p.m.;
Sat./Sun. 10 a.m. to 8 p.m.

80 Potsdam

For those feeling in need of a break from the hectic pace of life in the city of Berlin, a trip to **Potsdam** just beyond the confines of the city can be throughly recommended. Here, the countryside is characterized by spacious lakes and undulating hills amid densely forested plains. One of the most remarkable Baroque towns in Germany, Potsdam was first mentioned in a charter from the reign of Otto III dating from 993. While, in the twelfth century, it was merely the site of a German fortress, the town attained prominence in 1660 when it became a residence of the Prince Elector. From this time onward, the development of the town was decisively influenced by the Hohenzollerns, whose lavish buildings included numerous castles, palaces, hunting lodges and summer houses, as well as the summer residence, **Sanssouci Castle**. Although much of the earlier charm and beauty of Potsdam was irrevocably lost as a result of damage incurred in the Second World War, its remaining architectural splendour more than justifies a prolonged visit. For example, in the center of the town close to many small officer's houses, we can find the Baroque Brandenburg Gate, which was built by Gonthard in 1770 using a Roman triumphal arch as his model. Also, the 53-meter-high dome of the Nikolai Church is a distinctive feature of the Potsdam skyline. This church was built between 1831 and 1837 according to plans by K. F. Schinkel to replace a Baroque church destroyed by a fire. The Nikolai Church was so severely damaged in the Second World War that it was only after almost 35 years of restoration work that it could finally be reopened in 1981. Another outstanding feature of the town is the Dutch Quarter (Holländisches Viertel). Built of rough brickwork and complete with canal and gabled houses, this quarter was intended for immigrant Dutch mercenaries of the army of Frederick I (1640–88). A further curious building in the center of Potsdam is the waterworks of Sanssouci, which has the striking form of a Moorish domed mosque. Commissioned by Frederick William IV after a trip to the Orient, the "mosque" conceals the waterworks and pumps needed to operate the fountains in the gardens of Sanssouci.

The Chinese Teahouse in the gardens of Sanssouci.

Although the town of Potsdam itself is interesting enough, the main reason why so many visitors come here is Sanssouci Castle with its spacious gardens and remarkable Baroque buildings. Situated at the summit of a steep hill with vineyards, the Rococo-style castle surmounting six large terraces was designed for Frederick II by Georg Wenzelslaus von Knobelsdorff. The "parterre" located below the restored terraces comprises a large pool ornamented on all sides with marble statues. As on the exterior of the building, the decoration of the interior, with its rocaille ornament, reliefs, paintings and gold-, silver- and marquetry-work give some idea of the expenditure that was laavished on this castle. It should be remembered that the castle was not intended for the royal family, but rather just for a single person – Frederick II. It can be seen that, even in his private sphere, the king expected an extraordinary level of comfort and convenience. For example, in Frederick's private library, virtually the only materials considered worthy of use were those of exceptional costliness or rarity, with gilded bronze or cedarwood seemingly representing the "bare minimum" with regard to suitability.

The **park and gardens** of Sanssouci are characterized by their variety, embracing lawns, wooded areas and gardens laid out in various "national styles," including Dutch, Sicilian and nordic gardens.

A particular attraction is the **"Dutch Windmill"** of the so-called **"miller of Sanssouci"**, who so the story goes, in spite of great promises, was not prepared to leave the land that had already been incorporated into the plans of the royal architects. How exactly this story ended, one can only guess; however, it is known that, within a few weeks of the dispute between the miller and the royal authorities, the "miller of Sanssouci" was neither seen nor heard of again. To the south-west of the castle not far from the large fountain, we come to the **Chinese Teahouse**, which was built in 1757 by Büring. Also to the south-west of Sanssouci Castle, there is **Charlottenhof Castle**, which was built for Crown Prince Frederick William. The work of K.F. Schinkel, it is modeled on the style of classical Ita-

The terraced garden of Sanssouci.

lian country villas. Another small castle, the **Cecilienhof**, became internationally famous in July/August, as it was here that, between 17th July and 2nd August, the **Potsdam Conference** took place, which resulted in the agreement of the same name between the four Allied Powers (USSR, USA, Great Britain and France) concerning the future of Germany. The most important section of this agreement was the resolution to destroy German Fascism and to punish the main war criminals.

To the south of Potsdam in the suburb Potsdam-Babelsberg are located the once-famous **UFA** (later, **DEFA**) **Film Studios**. It was here, in 1930, that the legendary actress, Marlene Dietrich, played the leading role in the film, "The Blue Angel."

Tips and Information

Berlin Marketing GmbH
BTM Hotline:
Tel. 030–250025
Fax 030–2500

Europa Center/Eingang Budapester Str.
Brandenburger Tor/Südflügel

Info Points:
Flughafen Tegel
Dresdner Bank/Ecke Unter den Linden

Important Telephone Numbers:
Pharmacy (all-night service): 01189
Emergency Medical Services: 310031
Red Cross Rescue Service: 85005/19222
Fire Brigade / Doctor on Emergency
Call: 112
In Case of Poisoning: 3023022
Police: 110
Emergency Dental Service: 89004333

Embassies and Consulates:
Australia
10623 Berlin, Uhlandstr. 181,
Tel: 8800880
Austria
10963 Berlin, Wilhelmstr. 5,
Tel: 6093865
Belgium
13187 Berlin, Esplanade 13,
Tel: 4459188
Denmark
10117 Berlin, Unter den Linden 41,
Tel: 250010
France
13469 Berlin, Rue Montesquieu 31,
Tel: 4143072
Great Britain
10117 Berlin, Unter den Linden 32,
Tel: 201840
Italy
10785 Berlin, Hiroshimastr. 1,
Tel: 2611591
Japan
10195 Berlin, Wachtelstr. 8, Tel: 8327026
Russia
10117 Berlin, Unter den Linden 36,
Tel: 2291110
Spain
10787 Berlin, Lichtensteinallee 1,
Tel: 2616081
Sweden
10709 Berlin, Kurfürstendamm 151,
Tel: 8917091
Switzerland
10557 Berlin, Fürst-Bismarck-Str. 4,
Tel: 3904000
USA
10117 Berlin, Neustädtische Kirchstr. 4,
Tel: 2385174

Railway Stations:
Lichtenberg, Tel: 2970
Main Station (Hauptbahnhof)
Tel: 20075
Zoologischer Garten, Tel: 29749350
Schönefeld, Tel: 29729517

Airports:
East Berlin:
Schönefeld, Tel: 60910
West Berlin:
Tegel, Tel: 41011
Tempelhof, Tel: 69510

Guided Tours of Berlin:
Most tours of Berlin begin and end at
the following places: Alexanderplatz,
the Brandenburg Gate, the Main Railway Station (Hauptbahnhof), the Kurfürstendamm and Breitscheidplatz.
The following companies offer bus tours
of the city:
BBS Berliner Bären Stadtrundfahrt
Ltd., Rankestr. 35, Tel. 2148790:
start in the Kurfürstendamm on the
corner of Rankestrasse, on Breitscheidplatz, or in front of the Forum Hotel on
Alexanderplatz.
Berolina Stadtrundfahrten, Meinekestr. 3,
Tel. 88220991: start at Kurfürstendamm 220 on the corner of Meineke-
strasse, or at the Radisson Plaza Hotel
in Karl-Liebknecht-Strasse.
BVB Stadtrundfahrten: start and ticket
purchase in Kurfürstendamm 225, Tel.
8859880.
BVG (Berliner Verkehrs-Betriebe). City
tour in a historic double-decker bus,
Tel. 2560; daily in summer on the hour
from 11 a.m. to 4 p.m., in winter only at
weekends at 11 a.m. and 1 and 3 p.m.
Start at Breitscheidplatz; tickets can be
purchased on the bus.

Culture and Theaters:
Berliner Ensemble: Bertolt-Brecht-
Platz 1, Mon.–Sat. 11 a.m. to 6 p.m.,
Tel. 28408155
Brecht House Berlin: Chausseestr. 125,
Tues.–Fri. 10 to 12 a.m., Tel. 2829916
Comic Opera: Behrenstr. 55–57,
Mon.–Fri. 12 a.m. to 5:30 p.m.,
Tel. 20260360
French Cultural Center: Unter den
Linden 37, Mon.–Fri. 11 a.m. to 7 p.m.
Friedrichstadtpalais: Friedrichstr. 107,
Tues.–Sat. 1 to 3:30 p.m.,
Tel. 28466474
German State Opera: Unter den
Linden 7, Mon.–Sat. 10 a.m. to 8 p.m.,
Tel. 20354555

German Theater and Kammerspiele:
Schumannstr. 13a, Mon.–Fri. 10 a.m. to
5 p.m., Tel. 28441221222
Maxim Gorky Theater: Am Festungs-
graben 2, Mon.–Sat. 1 to 6:30 p.m.,
Tel. 20221129
Metropol Theater: Friedrichstr.
101–102, Mon.–Sat. 10 a.m. to 6 p.m.,
Tel. 202460 (extension 117)
Philharmonie: Matthäikirchstr. 1,
Tel. 2628515
Theater of the West: Kantstr. 12,
Tel. 8822888

Museums, Galleries and Castles:
Bauhaus Archive: Klingelhöferstr. 14,
daily (except Tues.) 10 a.m. to 5 p.m.,
Tel. 2540020
Berlin Museum: Lindenstr. 14
(owing to renovation, closed until
1998) Tel. 2380900
Bröhan Museum: Schloss-Str. 1a,
Tues.–Sun. 10 a.m. to 6 p.m.,
Tel. 3214029
Charlottenburg Castle: Spandauer
Damm, daily 9 a.m. to 5 p.m.,
Tel. 320911
Egyptian Museum: Schloss-Str. 70,
Mon.–Thurs. 9 a.m. to 5 p.m.,
Sat./Sun. 10 a.m. to 5 p.m.,
Tel. 320911
German Broadcasting Museum:
Hammerskjöldplatz 1, Weds.–Mon.
10 a.m. to 5 p.m., Tel. 3028186
German Historical Museum: Unter den
Linden 2, Thurs.–Tues. 10 a.m. to 6
p.m., Tel. 215020
Haus am Checkpoint Charlie: Fried-
richstr. 44, daily 9 a.m. to 10 p.m.,
Tel. 2511031
Huguenot Museum: Gendarmenmarkt,
Tues.–Sun. 12 a.m. to 5 p.m.,
Tel. 2291760
Käthe Kollwitz Museum: Fasanen-
str. 24, Weds.–Mon. 11 a.m. to 6 p.m.,
Tel. 8825210
Martin Gropius Building: Strese-
mannstr. 110, Tues.–Sun. 10 a.m. to
10 p.m.
National Gallery (East): Bodestr. 1–3,
Weds.–Sun. 9 a.m. to 5 p.m.,
Tel. 209050
New National Gallery: Potsdamer Str.
50, Tues.–Fri. 9 a.m. to 5 p.m.,
Sat./Sun. 10 a.m. to 5 p.m.,
Tel. 2666
Old Museum: Bodestr. 1–3, Mon.–Fri.
9 to 12 a.m. and 1 to 5 p.m.,
Tel. 209050
Pergamon and Bode Museums:
Bodestr. 1–3, Tel. 20905431
Schinkel Museum: Werderstr., Tues.–
Sun. 9 a.m. to 5 p.m., Tel. 2081323

Churches and Memorials:
Church of St. Mary: Karl-Liebknec.
Str., Tel. 2424467
Kaiser William Church of Remem-
brance: Breitscheidplatz,
Tel. 3911301
Memorial in the House of the Wannsee
Conference: Am Grossen Wannsee
56–58, Tues.–Fri. 10 a.m. to 6 p.m.;
Sat./Sun. 2–6 p.m., Tel. 80500126
Memorial of German Resistance:
Stauffenbergstr. 13–14, Mon.–Fri.
9 a.m. to 6 p.m., Sat./Sun. 9 a.m. to
1 p.m., Tel. 26542202
New Synagogue: Oranienburger Str. 39,
Tel. 28401250
Parochial Church: Klosterstr. 67,
Tel. 2475950
Plötzensee Memorial: Hüttigpfad, daily
8 a.m. to 6 p.m., Tel. 3443226
Sophienkirche: Grosse Hamburger
Str. 28, Tel. 2823232

Others:
Archenhold Observatory: Alt-Treptow 1,
Mon.–Thurs. 2 to 5:30 p.m.,
Fri.–Sun. 2 to 7:30 p.m.
House of the Cultures of the World:
John-Foster-Dulles-Allee 10,
Tel. 397870
Müggel Tower: In den Müggelbergen,
Mon.–Fri. 10 a.m. to 7 p.m.; Sat./Sun.
10 a.m. to 8 p.m.
Radio Tower: Messedamm 11, daily
10 a.m. to 9:30 p.m.
State Library (I) (East): Unter den
Linden 8, Mon.–Fri. 9 a.m. to 9 p.m.;
Sat. 9 a.m. to 5 p.m., Tel. 20150
State Library (II) (West): Potsdamer
Str. 33, Mon.–Fri. 9 a.m. to 9 p.m.;
Sat. 9 a.m. to 5 p.m., Tel. 2623701
Television Tower: Panoramastr. 1a, daily
9 a.m. to 12 p.m., Tel. 5348080
Urania: An der Urania 17, Tel. 2189091
Zoological Garden/Aquarium: Buda-
pester Str., daily 9 a.m. to 6 p.m.

Swimming Pools, Saunas, Indoor
Tennis Courts:
Sport und Erholungszentrum (SEZ),
Landsberger Allee 77, Tel: 422830
blub Badeparadies, Buschkrugallee 64,
Tel: 6066060
Stadtbad Charlottenburg, Krummestr.
10, Tel: 34303241
Solf-Sauna, Bundesallee 187,
Tel: 8545014
Thermen am Europacenter, Nürn-
bergerstr. 7, Tel: 2616031
Tennis in der City, Franklinstr. 9,
Tel: 39190174
Tennis-Center-Tegel, Flohrstr. 11–21,
Tel: 4346666

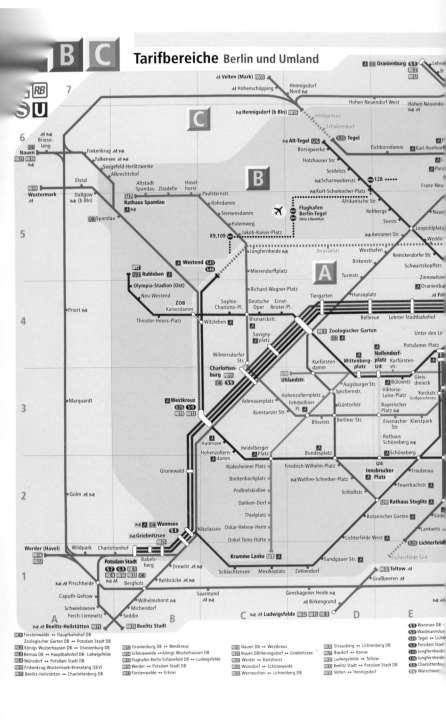

Tarifbereiche Berlin und Umland

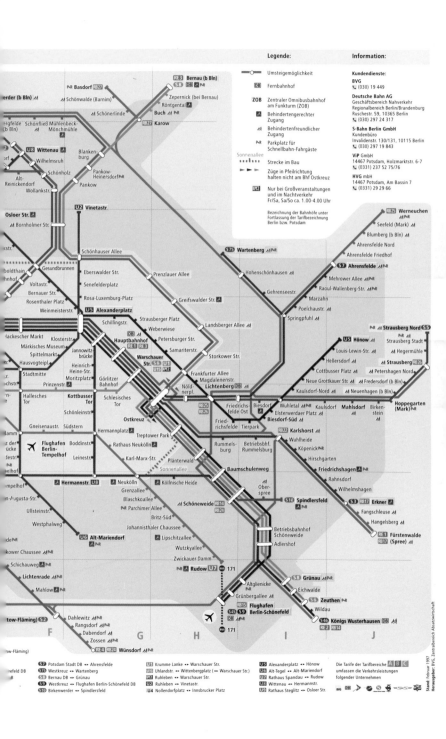

Index